URBAN HIKES WASHINGTON

HELP US KEEP THIS GUIDE UP TO DATE

Every effort has been made by the authors and editors to make this guide as accurate and useful as possible. However, many things can change after a guide is published—trails are rerouted, regulations change, facilities come under new management, and so forth.

We would love to hear from you concerning your experiences with this guide and how you feel it could be improved and kept up to date. While we may not be able to respond to all comments and suggestions, we'll take them to heart, and we'll also make certain to share them with the authors. Please send your comments and suggestions to the following address:

Globe Pequot Press
Reader Response/Editorial Department
PO Box 480
Guilford, CT 06437

Or you may e-mail us at:

editorial@GlobePequot.com

Thanks for your input, and happy trails!

URBAN HIKES
WASHINGTON

A GUIDE TO THE STATE'S GREATEST
URBAN HIKING ADVENTURES

Brandon Fralic and Rachel Wood

FALCONGUIDES

GUILFORD, CONNECTICUT

FALCONGUIDES®

An imprint of The Rowman & Littlefield Publishing Group, Inc.
4501 Forbes Blvd., Ste. 200
Lanham, MD 20706
www.rowman.com

Falcon and FalconGuides are registered trademarks and Make Adventure Your Story is a trademark of The Rowman & Littlefield Publishing Group, Inc.

Distributed by NATIONAL BOOK NETWORK

Photos by Brandon Fralic and Rachel Wood
Maps by The Rowman & Littlefield Publishing Group, Inc.

British Library Cataloguing in Publication Information available

Library of Congress Cataloging-in-Publication Data available

ISBN 978-1-4930-4783-3 (paper: alk. paper)
ISBN 978-1-4930-4784-0 (electronic)

♾™ The paper used in this publication meets the minimum requirements of American National Standard for Information Sciences—Permanence of Paper for Printed Library Materials, ANSI/NISO Z39.48-1992.

The authors and The Rowman & Littlefield Publishing Group, Inc. assume no liability for accidents happening to, or injuries sustained by, readers who engage in the activities described in this book.

This book is dedicated to our loved ones: Create Something Beautiful.

CONTENTS

Overview

BEFORE YOU HIT THE TRAIL

"Man did not weave the web of life, he is merely a strand in it. Whatever he does to the web, he does to himself."

—Chief Seattle

It's hard to argue against calling Washington the Evergreen State. The western half experiences frequent rainfall, resulting in dense conifer-filled forests. And even though it's considerably drier, the eastern half of the state is blanketed by the green of agriculture. The Columbia Basin is a patchwork of grape vineyards, fruit tree orchards, and green swaying Timothy hay.

You'll also find ample green spaces within Washington's biggest cities. Inspired by the City Beautiful Movement influenced by the Olmsted Brothers, the state's most celebrated urban public spaces retain an emerald hue. From perennial favorites like Washington Park Arboretum to hidden gems like Lake Sacajawea Park, many city parks were planned to echo Washington's natural beauty, flowing into the urbanity of the city surrounding them.

Outside of the dense Greater Seattle Area and sprawl along the I-5 corridor, cities become islands of modernity—surrounded by untamed swaths of forest and fertile valleys in the west, or scablands and rolling prairies to the east. This abundance of nature is what draws many transplants to Washington. However, harm has come to the environment due to human influence. Restoration is happening across the state—from the clean-up of once-industrial shorelines to rerouting trails and stopping erosion in fragile prairie lands. The green spaces just outside our cities that we flock to for recreation are also places balanced on the line between wild and tamed.

DEFINING URBAN HIKES

The urban hikes in this guide showcase the diversity of Washington State. From waterfront walks along rivers, creeks, lakes, and saltwater shorelines to botanical gardens, nature preserves, and old-growth forests—there's a hike for every age, ability, and interest in Washington. Typically, these trails are found in city and county parks. They can also exist in state parks, national parks, and other public and private lands. Since most urban areas in Washington are near sea level or at relatively low elevation, urban hikes are generally accessible year round.

Urban hikes are defined by their ease of access. The hikes in this guide are located in or near (within 30 minutes drive of) the city. We won't send you out any pothole-filled forest roads to reach them. And once you're there, the whole family can participate. Most recommended trails are dog friendly, and many of our suggested hikes are as little as 2 miles round trip—a perfect introduction to the outdoors for little legs. Many urban trails are paved, allowing access for both strollers and wheelchairs. Finally, you'll often find amenities like restrooms, water, picnic areas, and playgrounds at the trailhead.

URBAN HIKES FOR TRAVELERS

Why write an urban hikes guidebook? We're glad you asked. Over the past several years, we have written about both hiking trails and travel; urban hikes are the ideal intersection of both. Some of the hikes in this book are old favorites from two lifetimes spent wandering Washington, while others are new discoveries made during our research. The cities that host these hikes make great travel destinations, ideal for a quick stopover or long weekend away.

To aid in your travels, we've included some of our favorite stops near the trailhead—from eateries and taprooms to nearby accommodations. Just like urban hikes themselves, this guidebook is a bit of a hybrid: part traditional hiking guide, part travel companion. These hikes are just as ideal for after-work exercise as they are a supplement to your Washington road trip travels. Need a leg stretch during a long drive across the state? We've got you covered.

WEATHER

Contrary to popular belief, it doesn't *always* rain in Washington. The western half of the state (west of the Cascade Mountains) is generally the wettest, with somewhere in the ballpark of 66 inches of rainfall per year, on average. Keep in mind that this number is an average, skewed heavily by the massive amount of rainfall received along the Olympic Peninsula. Seattle sees closer to 35–40 inches of annual rain. Central and Eastern Washington receive roughly half (or less) the annual rainfall of Seattle. So if you're looking for a drier climate, head east!

Western Washington enjoys cooler summers and milder winters than Central and Eastern Washington. Summers on the west side, which includes Seattle and Puget Sound, are sublime, while mid-summer in Spokane can be downright stifling. Therefore, the best time for urban hiking in Washington depends on which part of the state you're in. While wetter, the western half of the state is generally hikeable year round. In Central and Eastern Washington, shoulder season (spring and fall) are most favorable.

Always check current weather conditions before setting out on a hike. You'll find accurate, up-to-date forecasts at the National Weather Service website: www.weather.gov.

FLORA AND FAUNA

The Cascade Mountains are the dividing line of Washington State. The mountain range separates the wet, temperate western side from the drier, continental-like climate of Eastern Washington. It's no wonder that each side of Washington State has its own cast of plants and animals that call the area home.

Western Washington, hit frequently by Pacific Ocean-fueled rain showers, is home to moss-covered forests of cedar, hemlock, and Douglas fir. Along its coastline you may spy a spotted harbor seal, or (with some luck) the dorsal fin of a Southern Resident orca. River otters, beavers, and croaking frogs inhabit the wetlands and rivers here.

Eastern Washington experiences true seasons—scorching summers and freezing winters. Quail and magpies burst from sagebrush in a flurry of feathers, while western rattlesnakes may warm themselves on the sunbaked trails. You might even catch sight of a skunk, ambling through tall grass. In the spring, hillsides burst into bloom with bright yellow arrowleaf balsamroot and purple lupine.

A good rule of thumb to keep in mind during any animal encounter or sighting: if the animal is changing its behavior (a rattlesnake starts to coil, a Canadian goose hisses at you) then you are too close. Give them space, and respect that you are a visitor to their home.

Urban trails don't always offer the best representation of "native" Washingtonian plants. Many of the trails in this book cross through botanical collections and city parks. These green spaces are curated and manicured by humans, for humans. Of course, this is not the case for all the trails found in these pages: many hikes explore areas of old-growth and second-growth forests, which are better representations of Washington's wild side.

ACCESS AND REGULATIONS

Washington is made up of a patchwork of public lands. According to the Washington Public Lands Inventory, city, county, state, and federal lands make up 19.8 million acres—about 43 percent of the state's total acreage. That's a whole lot of public land, and each agency has different access requirements. We've listed fees and parking pass requirements under the "Fees and permits" section for each hike. Most urban hikes in this guide are located in city and county parks, which generally do not require a parking pass (unless otherwise noted). We've only included one urban hike in a national park (Hike #2, Spruce Railroad Trail in Olympic National Park). At the time of writing, no parking pass was required at the Spruce Railroad Trailhead.

That leaves state lands, which include Washington State Parks and Department of Natural Resources (DNR)-owned properties. On these lands, you'll need a Discover Pass ($10/day or $30/year) for parking. Discover Passes can be obtained online (www .discoverpass.wa.gov), at state park offices and kiosks, and from any of nearly 600 recreational license vendors where state fishing and hunting licenses are sold. You can also take advantage of state park free days, during which no pass or fee is required for parking. Free days usually fall on holidays and are listed on the Discover Pass website.

It's imperative to respect our state's public and private lands. Always stay on-trail (avoid cutting switchbacks) and pack out everything that you pack in. Even biodegradable items should be properly disposed of—banana peels can take two years to decompose. Fortunately, most parks provide convenient garbage (and sometimes recycling) receptacles. Always practice Leave No Trace principles in the outdoors to keep our wild spaces wild. These seven principles include dispose of waste properly, leave what you find, respect wildlife, and be considerate of other visitors. Visit www.lnt.org to learn more.

HOW TO USE THIS GUIDE

The hikes are presented in an easy-to-read format with at-a-glance information at the start. Each hike description contains the following information:

Hike number and name: The hike number is also shown on the location map to help you visualize the general location of the hike. We've used the official, or at least the commonly accepted, name for a trail or hike. Loop hikes or other routes that use several trails are usually named for the main trail or for a prominent feature along the way.

Overview: Each hike is introduced with a **general description** of the hike, including special attractions.

Nearest town: This is the distance from the nearest town with at least a gas station and basic supplies.

Distance: This indicates the total distance of the hike in miles. Distances were carefully measured using the Gaia GPS mobile app. Hikes may be loops, which use a series of trails so that you never retrace your steps; out and back, which return along the same trails used on the way out; and lollipop, which are hikes with an out-and-back section leading to a loop.

Hiking time: This time in hours is necessarily based on average hiking times for a reasonably fit person. Non-hikers will take longer, and very fit, seasoned hikers will take less time.

Difficulty: All the hikes are rated as easy, moderate, or difficult, often with the reason for the rating. This is a subjective rating, but in general easy hikes can be done by nearly anyone and take a couple of hours at most. Because this guide features urban hikes, most of the trails within are considered easy. Moderate hikes take a bit longer, and usually introduce a significant amount of elevation gain (500 feet or more). Difficult hikes are steep, climbing more than 750 feet.

Trail surface: Paved path, dirt, gravel, sand.

Water: Generally, hikers bring all the water they need from home. Since some hikers like to carry less water and refill along the way, water sources are listed for each hike.

Seasons: This is the recommended time to do the hike. The months listed are those when the trailhead is accessible and the trail snow free. The season may be longer or shorter in some years. Check local conditions if you have any doubts. Most of the trails in this urban hiking guide are accessible year round.

Other trail users: Some of the hikes are on trails shared with joggers, horses, or mountain bikes.

Canine compatibility: This section tells you if dogs are permitted or not, and whether they must be on a leash.

Land status: When hiking the trails described in this book, usually you'll be hiking in city parks, various categories of state lands, land trust preserves, and even private property. The status of the land sometimes affects access or rules for use.

Fees and permits: This section lists if a fee is required for trailhead parking.

Maps: The official park or trail map is listed for each hike. These maps can be accessed online, and in many cases are available in hard copy form at the city or park visitor center. Users can also visit natgeomaps.com to locate USGS and Trails Illustrated maps for each hike.

Trail contacts: This section lists the name and contact information for the land-management agency that has jurisdiction over the hike. It's always a good idea to contact the agency before you hike to learn of trail closures, ongoing construction projects, or other unusual conditions.

Finding the trailhead: These driving directions are given in miles from the nearest large town or main highway for all of the hikes, followed by the GPS coordinates of the trailhead.

The hike: In this narrative, the hike is described in detail, along with interesting natural and human history. The description uses references to landmarks rather than distances wherever possible, since distances are listed under key points.

Miles and directions: This is a listing of key points along the hike, including trail junctions and important landmarks. You should be able to follow the route by reference to this section; however, the key points are not a substitute for thoroughly reading the hike narrative before taking the trip. Distances are given from the start of the hike in miles.

TRAIL FINDER

	BEST PHOTOS	FAMILY FRIENDLY	WATER FEATURES	DOG FRIENDLY	FINDING SOLITUDE
01 Port Angeles Waterfront Trail		•	•	•	
02 Spruce Railroad Trail	•	•	•	•	•
03 Chetzemoka Trail		•	•	•	
04 Fort Worden Loop	•	•	•	•	•
05 Dickerson Falls Trail	•	•	•	•	
06 Lake Padden Loop		•	•	•	
07 South Bay Trail	•	•	•	•	
08 Whatcom Creek Trail	•	•	•	•	
09 Guemes Channel - Ship Harbor Trails	•	•	•	•	
10 Deception Pass Headlands	•	•	•	•	•
11 Padilla Bay Shore Trail		•	•	•	•
12 Meadowdale Beach Park		•	•	•	•
13 North Creek Park		•	•	•	•
14 Sammamish River Trail		•	•	•	
15 Washington Park Arboretum	•	•	•	•	
16 Alki Trail	•	•	•	•	
17 Discovery Park Loop	•	•	•	•	•
18 Wilburton Hill Park	•	•	•		
19 Mercer Slough Heritage Loop		•	•	•	•
20 Snoqualmie Falls Trail	•	•	•	•	
21 Gene Coulon Park	•	•	•		
22 Dune Peninsula to Point Defiance Park	•	•	•	•	
23 Billy Frank Jr. Nisqually National Wildlife Refuge	•	•	•		•
24 Capitol Lake Loop	•	•	•	•	
25 Ellis Cove Trail	•	•	•	•	•
26 Lake Sacajawea Park	•	•	•	•	

	BEST PHOTOS	FAMILY FRIENDLY	WATER FEATURES	DOG FRIENDLY	FINDING SOLITUDE
27 Columbia River Renaissance Trail		•	•	•	
28 Round Lake Loop		•	•	•	•
29 Yakima Greenway		•	•	•	•
30 Cowiche Canyon Trail	•	•	•	•	•
31 Blackbird Island	•	•	•	•	
32 Apple Capital Loop Trail	•	•	•	•	
33 Saddle Rock Trail	•	•		•	
34 Chelan River Gorge		•	•	•	•
35 Richland Riverfront Trail		•	•	•	
36 Bateman Island		•	•	•	•
37 Badger Mountain	•	•		•	•
38 Spokane River Walk Loop	•	•	•	•	
39 Bowl and Pitcher Loop	•	•	•	•	•
40 Dishman Hills Loop		•		•	•

MAP LEGEND

Municipal

≡⬡5⬡≡ Freeway

⇒(160)⇐ US Highway

⇒(105)⇐ State Road

≡≡≡ Local/County Road

⊏FR 318⊐ Unpaved/Forest Road

= = = = Gravel Road

▬▬▬ Forest Boundary

——— State/County Park Boundary

···—··· State Line

⊢——⊣ Railroad

•—•—•—• Utility Line

Trails

- - - - - Featured Trail

═══════ Featured Road

- - - - - Trail

Water Features

Body of Water

Marsh

Rapids

River/Creek

Waterfall

Land Features

ⅿⅿⅿⅿ Cliffs

Symbols

⦀⦀⦀ Boardwalk/Steps

⇌ Boat Launch

≍ Bridge

▲ Campground

① Featured Trailhead

❓ Information Station

■ Point of Interest

🅿 Parking

▲ Peak/Elevation

🎪 Picnic Area

🚻 Restroom

🔭 Scenic View

🗼 Lighthouse

○ Town

↗ Trail Arrows

⊢==⊣ Tunnel

❓ Visitor Center

💧 Water

Tall conifers shade the curving trail, while salal blankets the forest floor.

OLYMPIC AND KITSAP PENINSULAS

At the far-flung western edge of Washington, the Olympic Peninsula is home to miles of Salish Sea and Pacific Ocean shoreline. This mountainous region is incredibly diverse in terms of geology and climate. The Olympic Mountains rise to nearly 8,000-foot heights, where active glaciers hang from Mount Olympus's slopes. The mountains, surrounding forestlands, and ocean beaches absorb 100-170 inches (8-14 feet) of rain annually from Pacific Ocean storms. It's no wonder the temperate rainforests of Olympic National Park are so lush! By the time rainclouds reach cities further inland on the peninsula, they're nearly tapped out.

We'll send you to the Olympic Peninsula's most accessible (and relatively dry) urban hubs. Both located in the Olympic Mountain rain shadow, the cities of Port Angeles and Port Townsend average only 20-30 inches of rainfall annually. Get a taste of the national park rainforest and glacially-carved Lake Crescent along the Spruce Railroad Trail. For a hike through history, walk Port Townsend's downtown waterfront on the Chetzemoka Trail. These and other easygoing urban hikes on the Olympic Peninsula reveal the region's natural beauty and human history—without the need to drive hours from the nearest city.

Further east across Hood Canal, the Kitsap Peninsula is even more accessible for urban dwellers. Basically a big island, Kitsap is connected to the mainland via bridges, ferry routes, and a narrow strip of land. Visitors can take the Bremerton ferry from downtown Seattle, or drive over the Tacoma Narrows Bridge for access to "the natural side of Puget Sound."

1 PORT ANGELES WATERFRONT TRAIL

Many know Port Angeles as the jumping-off point for Victoria, BC and Olympic National Park. But there's plenty to see in town, too! Take a stroll on the Waterfront Trail for an easygoing introduction to the sunny Olympic Peninsula.

Elevation gain: 50 feet
Distance: 2.4 miles out-and-back
Hiking time: 1–2 hours
Difficulty: Easy
Seasons: Year round
Trail surface: Paved path, boardwalk
Land status: City park
Nearest town: Port Angeles
Other users: Cyclists, joggers
Water availability: None

Canine compatibility: Dogs must remain on leash
Fees and permits: None
Map: ODT East Central - Olympic Discovery Trail: www .olympicdiscoverytrail.org/explore/ trail-segments/east-central
Trail contact: Port Angeles Parks and Recreation: (360) 417-4550
Trailhead GPS: N48.1204 W123.4308

FINDING THE TRAILHEAD

From US 101 (E Front Street), take N Lincoln Street one block north to E Rail-road Avenue. Turn left on Railroad Avenue and proceed to the Port Angeles Visitor Center (121 E Railroad Ave., Port Angeles, WA). Parking is available at several spots in downtown Port Angeles, including City Pier and a free 3-hour lot across Railroad Avenue from the visitor center. Begin your hike in front of the visitor center.

WHAT TO SEE

Sandwiched between Olympic National Park's Hurricane Ridge and the Salish Sea, Port Angeles offers some of the highest odds for a sunny seaside walk in Washington State. Because the largest city on the Olympic Peninsula is situated in the Olympic Mountain rain shadow, it receives significantly less rainfall—and more sunshine—than the wet western side of the Olympics. That's reason enough for Washingtonians and visitors alike to take in the city's charming downtown along the paved Waterfront Trail.

The Port Angeles Waterfront Trail extends west from the downtown waterfront, past the marina, and ends at the Coast Guard Station on Ediz Hook. However, much of this route requires walking along busy streets and through industrial areas. Our advice? Ediz Hook is best accessed by bike or car. Instead, take advantage of the Waterfront Trail's seamless transition into the greater Olympic Discovery Trail by heading east to experience a quieter seaside stroll.

From the Visitor's Center head first to the Port Angeles City Pier. You'll watch anglers of all ages throw out their lines or drop a crab pot or two. Climb up the observation tower for a postcard-ready view of the waterfront and the jagged outline of Hurricane Ridge in the distance. Watch for the Black Ball Ferry as it crosses the Strait of Juan de Fuca to and from Victoria, BC. Seals may be spotted bobbing offshore, and even Mount

Hurricane Ridge and the Olympic Mountains as seen from the observation tower on the City Pier.

Baker is visible on clear days. Colorful starfish cling to rocks beneath the pier—there's a lot to see if you take the time to observe.

Head back down the pier to meet back up with the trail on the south side of Feiro Marine Life Center (worth a stop, though there is an entrance fee). You'll pass by Hollywood Beach and a playground before walking east on the Waterfront Trail. The trail continues past the Red Lion Hotel before transitioning to a peaceful, tree-lined greenbelt. Welcome to the Olympic Discovery Trail. A multiuse, 130-mile long distance trail, the "ODT" stretches from Port Townsend along coastlines and through forests before ending at the Pacific Ocean in La Push, WA. This stretch through Port Angeles is one of the precious few located directly on the saltwater shoreline. The wide paved path is elevated from the gentle nudging of waves and shaded by overhanging trees. This mile is a peaceful one.

Once you reach the 9/11 Memorial Waterfront Park, head up the ramp to offer a moment of remembrance. The park's most important feature is an actual section of I-beam, recovered from Ground Zero in New York City. Also home to a life-sized harbor seal statue and tiered viewing platforms, the circular layout makes for an easy loop before heading back to downtown on the ODT. It is possible to continue east on the ODT of course, but the next section is best left to joggers and cyclists as it eventually turns away from the waterfront.

Upon returning to your starting point, continue west past the Black Ball Ferry dock towards Waterfront Park. This stretch offers the best views towards the end of Ediz Hook, a naturally occurring, 3-mile sand spit. On your way back from the park, we suggest exploring The Landing's many shops, and perhaps stopping in at The Olympic Coast Discovery Center to learn more about protecting the waters of the area and the animals that call this section of the Salish Sea their home.

Going Further: Since the Olympic Discovery Trail spans over 50 miles in either direction, it's possible to continue for as long as you like. We suggest bikes to avoid road-walking through less scenic areas.

MILES AND DIRECTIONS

0.0 Take the sidewalk east down Railroad Avenue from the visitor center. Turn left (north) at City Pier and walk to the end of the pier.

0.2 Reach the pier viewing tower, and ascend its steps for sea-to-summit views. Then walk south through the park to reach Hollywood Beach, a playground, and the Olympic Discovery Trail.

0.4 Walk east on the signed Olympic Discovery Trail.

1.0 Reach a trail junction at 9/11 Memorial Waterfront Park. Continue straight on the ODT to a second junction.

1.1 Turn right into 9/11 Memorial Waterfront Park.

1.2 Turn right to loop back to the ODT through the park. Retrace your steps to the visitor's center.

1.9 Back at the visitor's center, continue west on Railroad Avenue to enter Waterfront Park. Make a short loop through the park before returning to your vehicle.

PORT ANGELES WATERFRONT TRAIL

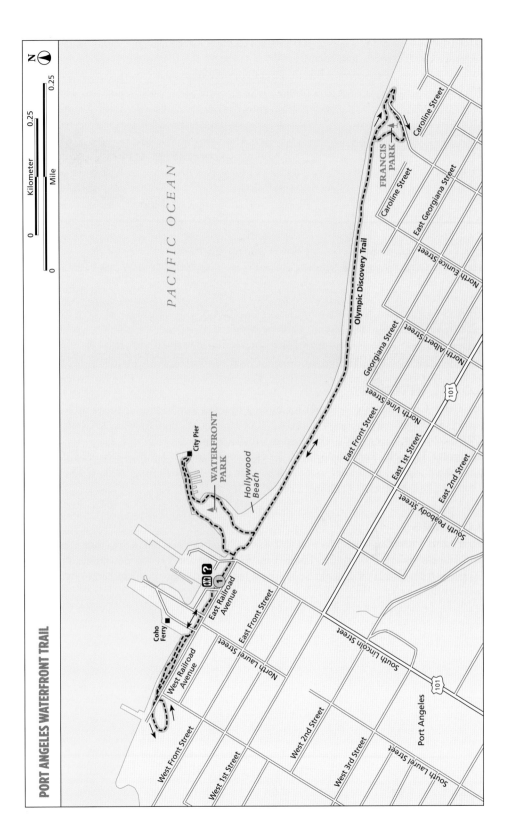

N

Kilometer
0   0.25   0.25

Mile
0   0.25

PACIFIC OCEAN

City Pier

WATERFRONT PARK

Hollywood Beach

Coho Ferry

West Railroad Avenue

East Railroad Avenue

West Front Street

West 1st Street

West 2nd Street

West 3rd Street

North Laurel Street

East Front Street

South Laurel Street

South Lincoln Street

Port Angeles

101

Olympic Discovery Trail

East Front Street

North Vine Street

Georgiana Street

North Albert Street

North Eunice Street

Caroline Street

East Georgiana Street

Caroline Street

FRANCIS PARK

East 1st Street

East 2nd Street

South Peabody Street

101

A wide, paved path, the Waterfront Trail is a section of the long distance Olympic Discovery Trail.

LOCAL INTEREST

La Belle Creperie: An ideal spot for brunch or a late lunch; enjoy a menu of both savory and sweet crepe options. Address: 222 N Lincoln St., Port Angeles, WA; Phone: (360) 452-9214; Web: www.facebook.com/LaBelleCreperie/

Songoku Hibachi and Sushi: With an expansive menu of Japanese-style favorites, Songoku is a lively and healthy spot to fill up after a day of adventuring. Address: 134 W Front St., Port Angeles, WA; Phone: (360) 477-4315

LODGING

Red Lion Port Angeles: The only full-service hotel in town offers oceanside views and complimentary bike rentals. Located on the Waterfront Trail in downtown Port Angeles. Address: 221 N Lincoln St., Port Angeles, WA; Phone: (360) 452-9215; Web: www.redlion.com

2 SPRUCE RAILROAD TRAIL

Spruce Railroad Trail offers a taste of Olympic National Park's stunning waters, mountains, and lush evergreen rainforest—all within half an hour's drive of Port Angeles. Bring the whole family on this easy, yet rewarding nature walk.

Elevation gain: 160 feet
Distance: 2.4-mile lollipop
Hiking time: 1-2 hours
Difficulty: Easy
Seasons: Year round
Trail surface: Paved (Trail is closed for construction as of March 2020 and will reopen in the fall of 2020.)
Land status: National Park
Nearest town: Port Angeles
Other users: Cyclists, joggers

Water availability: None
Canine compatibility: Dogs must remain on leash
Fees and permits: None
Map: Lake Crescent Area Brochure - Olympic National Park: www.nps.gov/olym/planyourvisit/lake-crescent-area-brochure.htm
Trail contact: Olympic National Park: (360) 565-3130
Trailhead GPS: N48.0933 W123.8027

FINDING THE TRAILHEAD

 From downtown Port Angeles (intersection of Front Street and Lincoln Street), drive south on US 101 West (Lincoln Street) toward Forks. After 16.2 miles, turn right onto E Beach Road. Drive 3.2 miles, then turn left to stay on E Beach Road. Continue 0.8 miles to the signed trailhead parking lot.

WHAT TO SEE

Beginning at the signed trailhead, walk south along Spruce Railroad Trail. Previously a gravel path, the Spruce Railroad Trail will be paved when it reopens in the fall of 2020. Why pave a perfectly good nature trail? Accessibility. Spruce Railroad is part of the greater Olympic Discovery Trail, which runs 130 miles from Port Townsend to the Pacific Ocean (see Hike #1). According to the National Park Service, paving and other improvements along the Spruce Railroad section will establish "a universally accessible, multipurpose trail to be shared by hikers, bicyclists, equestrians and people traveling in wheelchairs."

Originally built to harvest the trail's namesake Sitka spruce in 1918, this rails-to-trails corridor is lush with life—an easy introduction to Olympic National Park not too far from the city. Pass beneath mossy maple trees on the wide, swordfern-lined path. Whether you find gravel or pavement underfoot, the grade is gentle as it traces the toe of Pyramid Mountain. At 0.4 miles the trail reaches a high point of 675 feet before sloping back down to the lakeshore.

Continue along a relatively flat 0.5 miles to McFee Tunnel. Previously closed to the public, this 450-foot-long tunnel was restored in 2017. Walk through the darkness if you dare! Kids (and perhaps adults, too) may feel more comfortable bringing a flashlight along. Soon you'll see the light at the end of the tunnel and pop out on the other side. You can continue south on the Spruce Railroad Trail from here (see Going Further), but we suggest hanging a left to access the Devil's Punchbowl.

Traverse the old Spruce Railroad on this rails-to-trails hike along Lake Crescent.

A short distance from the tunnel you'll reach the footbridge over Devil's Punchbowl. A popular summer swimming hole, the picturesque punchbowl makes a good destination for relaxing beside Lake Crescent. Peer deep into the lake's crystalline blue-green waters. Reaching depths of 624 feet, Lake Crescent is the second-deepest lake in Washington (after Lake Chelan). On clear days you can peer out at the Olympic Mountains across the lake, though low-hanging clouds often obscure them. Head back to the trailhead once you've had your fill.

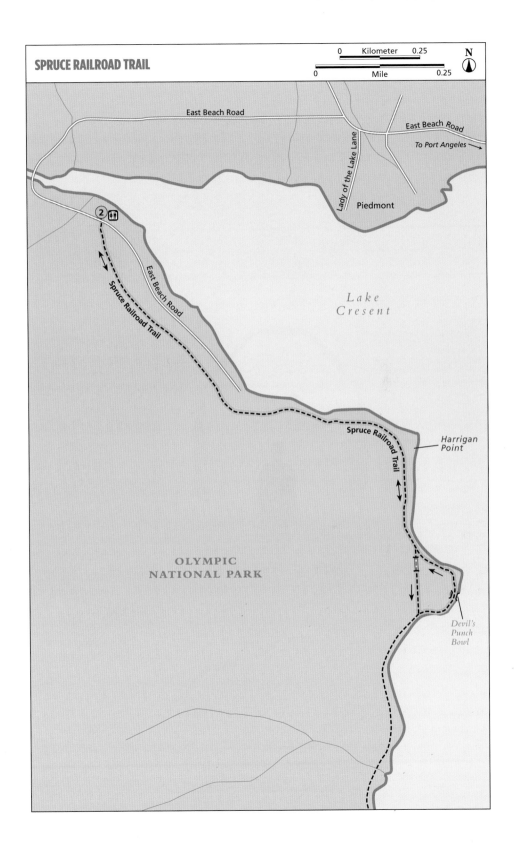

SPRUCE RAILROAD TRAIL

0   Kilometer   0.25

0   Mile   0.25

N

East Beach Road

East Beach Road

To Port Angeles →

Lady of the Lake Lane

Piedmont

2

Spruce Railroad Trail

East Beach Road

Lake Cresent

Spruce Railroad Trail

Harrigan Point

OLYMPIC NATIONAL PARK

Devil's Punch Bowl

The trail leads through the dark depths of a tunnel—
young hikers might appreciate a flashlight!

Going Further: From the south end of McFee Tunnel, Spruce Railroad Trail continues along the shoreline. At 2.7 miles from the trailhead you'll reach the Daley Rankin Tunnel. An additional mile of trail leads west from Daley Rankin Tunnel to Spruce Railroad Trail's western trailhead at the end of Camp David Jr. Road. From here, you can continue west on the Olympic Discovery Trail.

MILES AND DIRECTIONS

- **0.0** Hike south on the Spruce Railroad Trail.
- **1.0** Reach McFee Tunnel. Walk carefully through the tunnel (or take the bypass trail along the lake).
- **1.1** At the tunnel's end, turn left to take the lakeshore trail.
- **1.2** Reach a footbridge spanning Devil's Punchbowl. Continue across the bridge.
- **1.3** Back at the tunnel's north entrance, return the way you came.

LOCAL INTEREST

Storm King Ranger Station: For information on additional activities around Lake Crescent and the greater park, visit this nearby ranger station. Open summers only. Address: Lake Crescent Road, Port Angeles, WA (located right off US 101 at Lake Crescent Road); Phone: (360) 928-3380; Web: www.nps.gov/olym

LODGING

Red Lion Port Angeles: Conveniently located on the Port Angeles Waterfront and Olympic Discovery Trail in downtown Port Angeles. Offers complimentary bike rentals for guests! Address: 221 N Lincoln St., Port Angeles, WA; Phone: (360) 452-9215; Web: www.redlion.com

Log Cabin Resort: Stay just 1 mile from the Spruce Railroad trailhead on the shores of Lake Crescent. Address: 3183 E Beach Rd., Port Angeles, WA; Phone: (360) 928-3325; Web: www.olympicnationalparks.com

3 CHETZEMOKA TRAIL

Explore the Victorian Seaport of Port Townsend by taking a walk through history on the Chetzemoka Trail, where you'll discover the legacy of the S'Klallam people and their last chief, čičməhán.

Elevation gain: 200 feet
Distance: 3.2 miles out-and-back
Hiking time: 2 hours
Difficulty: Easy
Seasons: Year round
Trail surface: Paved path, sand
Land status: City park
Nearest town: Port Townsend
Other users: Cyclists
Water availability: None

Canine compatibility: Dogs must remain on leash
Fees and permits: None
Map: čičməhán Trail Map - Jamestown S'Klallam Tribe: www.tribalmuseum.jamestowntribe.org
Trail contact: Jamestown S'Klallam Tribe: (360) 681-4614
Trailhead GPS: N48.1221 W122.7564

FINDING THE TRAILHEAD

From the Port Townsend ferry terminal, drive east on Water Street for 0.5 miles. Turn left onto Monroe Street and drive 0.4 miles. Then turn right onto Blaine Street and continue 300 feet ahead to Jackson Street. Parking is available along Jackson Street at the entrance to Chetzemoka Park.

WHAT TO SEE

A historical walking route through downtown Port Townsend, the Chetzemoka Trail honors the legacy of the last chief of the S'Klallam tribe, čičməhán (pronounced Cheech-ma-han). Helping his people navigate the tense "Treaty" period, čičməhán is remembered for his forward-thinking leadership that prioritized communication and cooperation with European-American settlers. Using existing trails and sidewalks, Chetzemoka Trail is a collection of three different routes (3-mile, 6-mile, and 12-mile respectively), which guide you on a tour of 18 historic sites around Port Townsend.

The route we describe here will take you on a hike to explore the first nine sites on the route, including the historic downtown, a walk along the beach, and exploration of the city's oldest park. The trail begins at said park, Chetzemoka Park. When entering the park's main gate, you'll be greeted for the first time by what will become a familiar sight: the Chetzemoka Trail interpretive signs. The black metal outline of a S'Klallam salmon tops the maroon sign, making them easy to spot. Each sign weaves the story of čičməhán's life.

Chetzemoka Park is a beautiful green space on a bluff overlooking the Salish Sea, with views towards Mount Baker. Explore the manicured gardens, or have a picnic before setting out on the trail by hitting the beach! The next section of the trail follows the coastline south towards Point Hudson. If it happens to be high tide, you might have to scrap this beach section and continue southwest on Jackson Street.

At 0.6 miles along the shoreline, you'll reach Point Hudson before turning inland. From here, you'll need to keep on the lookout for another type of trail marker—a small red and white circle insignia that indicates the trail's route. These insignias are found embedded in the sidewalk at each major intersection, and appear on many signposts,

Each historical site along the trail has an interpretive sign, like this one seen in front of the Fowler Building.

keeping you on track between interpretive sites. If time allows, stop in at the Northwest Maritime Center to learn about Coast Salish canoe culture, and spend a moment admiring the Welcome Totem, carved and designed by local artisans in the S'Klallam tradition.

This is also your welcome to historic downtown Port Townsend. Water Street is the main thoroughfare, and can get downright crowded on sunny summer weekends. Keep an eye out for the Chetzemoka insignias in the sidewalks—a fun scavenger hunt for younger hikers—and follow them to discover the three other historic sites in the lower downtown area. Turn up Tyler Street and climb the staircase to Washington Street. Then get ready to climb! Washington Street is quite steep as it ascends the bluffs. But the views are gorgeous. Make sure to stop at the overlook sign for a view down to the ferry docks and the Salish Sea.

Continue on Washington Street until you come to the Post Office. The oldest federally constructed post office in the state, this grand structure housed the Customs House as well as the court when it was constructed. To honor čičməhán and his success in uniting the settlers and S'Klallam tribe, his face, and those of his two wives and older brother, are carved into the capital of the entrance columns. This fitting tribute, in a meeting of the two cultures, has an ideal vantage point over the town and seas below.

Going Further: From the Post Office you can continue north along the 3-mile loop back to Chetzemoka Park. However, this section of trail is less scenic on foot, as it goes through neighborhood streets. You can also head west on the 6-mile loop to access Kah Tai Lagoon Park.

The trail takes you through Point Hudson Marina, bustling with boats.

MILES AND DIRECTIONS

0.0 From the signed entrance to Chetzemoka Park, take the main trail down into the park. Walk northeast across the grassy lawn down to the fence.

0.1 Walk the fenceline south for beach access.

0.2 Reach the beach. Walk south along the shoreline toward Point Hudson.

0.6 At Point Hudson, turn inland (west) at the Chetzemoka Trail sign and walk through the RV Park. Turn right (north) on Hudson Street. Follow Chetzemoka Trail markers through the marina to Jefferson Street.

0.7 Turn left on Jefferson Street.

0.8 Turn left on Jackson Street.

0.9 Turn right on Water Street. Continue following Chetzemoka Trail markers southwest through downtown Port Townsend.

1.3 From Water Street, turn right on Tyler Street and ascend the stairs. Then turn left onto Washington Street.

1.6 Reach the Post Office on Washington Street. Turn around and retrace your steps to Chetzemoka Park. Alternatively, you can extend your walk via one of the loop trails (see Going Further).

The Jefferson County Courthouse is an iconic landmark on the skyline of the city, and is visited along the 6-mile-loop route of the Chetzemoka Trail.

LOCAL INTEREST

The In Between: Located on the mezzanine between a bookstore and Sirens Pub, The In Between is a slice of Deco cocktail elegance. Address: 823 Water St., Port Townsend, WA; Phone: (350) 379-2425; Web: theinbetweenpt.com

LODGING

Bishop Victorian Hotel: Historic downtown B&B featuring Victorian gardens, located along the Chetzemoka Trail. Breakfast is delivered to your room in a basket each morning. Address: 714 Washington St., Port Townsend, WA; Phone: (833) 254- 2469; Web: bishopvictorian.com

4 FORT WORDEN LOOP

From 200-foot blufftop views of the Salish Sea to saltwater shoreline access and decades of military history, Fort Worden offers endless opportunities for exploration. This easy loop provides a highlight reel of the park's most fascinating features.

Elevation gain: 230 feet
Distance: 2.3-mile loop
Hiking time: 1–2 hours
Difficulty: Easy
Seasons: Year round
Trail surface: Gravel, paved path
Land status: State park
Nearest town: Port Townsend
Other users: Cyclists, joggers
Water availability: Yes, at restrooms
Canine compatibility: Dogs must remain on leash

Fees and permits: Discover Pass required in designated lots (not required in Taps at the Guardhouse parking lot)
Map: Fort Worden Trail Map - Friends of Fort Worden: www .fwfriends.org/trailmaps
Trail contact: Fort Worden State Park Ranger Office: (360) 344-4412
Trailhead GPS: N48.1344 W122.7691

FINDING THE TRAILHEAD

From the Port Townsend ferry terminal, drive west on Water Street for 0.5 mile. Turn right onto Kearney Street, then drive 0.2 mile. Turn right onto Lawrence Street, then drive 0.2 miles. Turn left onto Walker Street. After 0.3 mile, Walker Street becomes Cherry Street. Continue 1 mile north on Cherry Street to enter Fort Worden State Park. After entering the park, continue 0.1 mile, then turn left on Eisenhower Avenue. Parking is available on the right, in the large lot next to Taps at the Guardhouse.

WHAT TO SEE

In the early 1900s, the "Triangle of Fire" (made up of Fort Worden, Fort Flagler, and Fort Casey) was constructed to thwart off potential Puget Sound invaders. Massive gun batteries were hidden in the hillside; nearly 1,000 troops trained and resided on the fort's grounds. This elaborate defense system was fortunately never needed. Today, the buildings that once housed military personnel have been repurposed across Fort Worden's campus, transforming the concrete complex into an educational and recreational state park full of military history. It's a captivating place for a windswept walk by the sea.

Fort Worden's winding trail network can be challenging to navigate without a map. Before setting out, pick up a free trail map from the trailhead kiosk or the visitor center (located at 200 Battery Way, in the old Fort Commander's Office Building).

From Taps at the Guardhouse, walk north along Fort Worden Way. Pass some old fuel pumps and the Madrona MindBody Institute (a space for massage and yoga workshops). While this initial section of road-walking isn't especially scenic, you'll soon enter the forest. Walking along the gated Battery Way West road means no vehicle traffic—just madrone trees, ferns, and wildlife to keep you company. When you come to Searchlight Road, walk out to Battery Walker for your first history lesson.

Once Fort Worden's most heavily used artillery emplacement, Battery Walker now sits quietly above the waters it was built to defend. Clamber over the battery steps, exploring

A large vessel as seen from the Bluff Trail at Fort Worden.

its cavernous interior if you dare. Then check out views north and east to Whidbey Island from the bluff. When you're ready to continue, retrace your steps to Searchlight Road and turn left (east) to explore the old searchlight tracks. Vertigo-inducing sea views await at the end of the line.

Back on Searchlight Road, depart from the pavement onto the gravel Bluff Trail. Situated on high bluffs and winding through coastal forest, this trail is the scenic highlight of the loop. Pass Battery Tolles—another worthy exploration site—before entering the woods and popping out near a breathtaking overlook. From here you can peer down on Point Wilson Lighthouse, some 200 feet below. It's possible to hike down to the lighthouse and beach via the steep Beach Campground Trail if you have the time. Of course, you can drive or bike down along Harbor Defense Way as well.

The next stop on your walk is Memory's Vault. A hauntingly beautiful art installation incorporating poetry and letters from Fort Worden's military history, it's worth visiting for a few minutes of quiet contemplation. From here you can head north up the Main Gun Line to Artillery Hill for more gun battery exploration. When you've had your fill of history, descend along the short but steep Madrona Trail to Alexanders Loop Road. Ahead, a large madrona tree stands sentinel before Alexander's Castle. Built in 1883, this red brick "castle" is the oldest building in the Fort Worden compound.

On the walk back to your car, you'll pass a number of notable buildings. The first belongs to Centrum, an arts organization that puts on musical performances, art festivals, and workshops throughout the year. Attendees often stay in the old barracks, or in the Victorian houses of Officers Row. You'll also pass the gift shop/visitor center and Coast Artillery Museum while strolling along the Parade Grounds and Officer's Row.

Back at Taps at the Guardhouse, consider having happy hour in the 1904-built barracks "for soldiers who breached military discipline, usually as a result of unauthorized activities in the rough and tumble taverns on Port Townsend's notorious Water Street." Shed your shackles!

MILES AND DIRECTIONS

0.0 From the parking lot, walk east towards Taps at the Guardhouse for access to restrooms and an informational kiosk. Take the sidewalk east along Eisenhower Avenue to Fort Worden Way and turn left (north).

0.2 Reach a junction with Battery Way. Continue straight (north) along the road.

0.3 Reach a gate and trailhead kiosk. Proceed through the gate onto Battery Way West.

0.6 Turn left onto Battery Walker Road.

0.7 Reach the junction with Searchlight Road. Take the short gravel path north for sea views and to check out Battery Walker, then return to the Searchlight Road junction.

0.8 Walk east on Searchlight Road. Take a detour to the left to check out an old searchlight track.

1.0 Turn left on the gravel Bluff Trail.

1.4 Reach an overlook above Point Wilson Lighthouse. Continue south on the Bluff Trail.

1.6 Turn left on Main Gun Line Road. Stay left on Battery Way East as you pass Memory's Vault.

1.7 Turn left and proceed down the steps on Madrona Trail.

1.8 Reach Alexanders Loop Road. Head left (south) along the road.

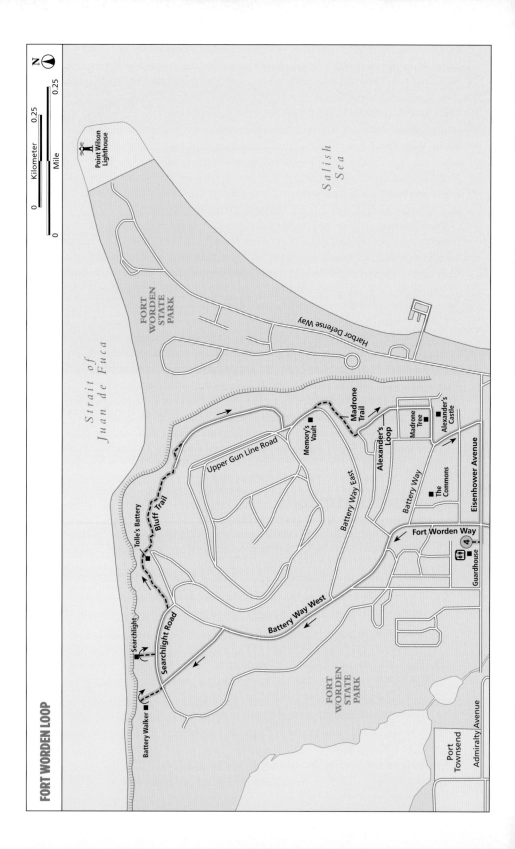

FORT WORDEN LOOP

N

Kilometer
0   0.25

0   0.25
Mile

Strait of
Juan de Fuca

Salish
Sea

Point Wilson
Lighthouse

FORT
WORDEN STATE
PARK

Harbor Defense Way

Battery Walker

Searchlight

Tolle's Battery

Bluff Trail

Searchlight Road

Upper Gun Line Road

Memory's Vault

Madrone Trail

Battery Way East

Alexander's Loop

Alexander's Castle

Madrone Tree

Battery Way

The Commons

Battery Way West

Fort Worden Way

Guardhouse

Eisenhower Avenue

FORT
WORDEN STATE
PARK

Port
Townsend

Admiralty Avenue

The fort now comes alive to host a variety of workshops and conferences, but some of the only permanent residents are blacktail deer.

1.9   Turn right in front of Alexander's Castle.

2.0   Turn left onto Battery Way.

2.1   Turn right onto Eisenhower Avenue. Continue back to your vehicle at Taps at the Guardhouse.

LOCAL INTEREST

Taps at the Guardhouse: Enjoy a bite to eat and perhaps a draft beer or two after your walk at Fort Worden. Address: 300 Eisenhower Ave., Port Townsend, WA; Phone: (360) 344-4400 Ext. 105; Web: www.fortworden.org/eat-drink

LODGING

Fort Worden Historic Lodgings: Stay at the state park! Several lodging options include cottages, Victorian vacation rentals, and campsites. Address: 200 Battery Way, Port Townsend, WA; Phone: (360) 344-4400; Web: www.fortworden.org/book-your-stay

5 DICKERSON FALLS TRAIL

Take a hike through a working tree farm to Dickerson Creek Falls, one of the most popular urban trail destinations near Bremerton.

Elevation gain: 240 feet
Distance: 2.4 miles out-and-back
Hiking time: 1 hour
Difficulty: Easy-moderate due to short, steep sections
Seasons: Year round
Trail surface: Dirt trail
Land status: Private land
Nearest town: Bremerton
Other users: Mountain bikers, joggers, equestrians, hunters

Water availability: None
Canine compatibility: Dogs must remain on leash
Fees and permits: None
Map: Ueland Tree Farm Trail Map: www.uelandtreefarm.com/assets/utf-map.pdf
Trail contact: Ueland Tree Farm: (253) 307-5900
Trailhead GPS: N47.5804 W122.7187

FINDING THE TRAILHEAD

From SR 3 near Bremerton, take the Austin Drive exit toward Kitsap Lake. Drive south on Austin Drive for 0.3 mile, then turn right onto Kitsap Way. Drive 0.6 mile, then take a slight left onto Northlake Way NW. Drive 0.6 mile, then take a sharp left onto Leber Lane NW. Continue 0.2 mile, up the gravel road to the signed trailhead on the right.

WHAT TO SEE

An active tree farm spanning over 2,200 acres of private land near Bremerton, Ueland Tree Farm is open to the public for nonmotorized recreation. That means you can hike, run, mountain bike, and even ride horses on the miles of trail and forest road here. The farm's most popular trail leads through evergreen forest to Dickerson Creek Falls, a small yet impressive waterfall worth the walk. Visit the falls year round for an excellent all-ages adventure.

The Ueland family purchased 1,700 acres from another tree farm here in 2004. Since then, they've taken steps to sustainably manage the land by establishing conservation easements that protect critical watershed areas including Chico Creek—the most productive salmon run in Kitsap County. This mix of environmental and social responsibility from private landowners is noteworthy. It's not often that we find ourselves hiking on private land in Washington State. Ueland Tree Farm is a unique recreation area, one that must be treated with the same respect as our public lands to ensure future access. Please tread lightly, and leave no trace in this special place.

A volunteer-built trailhead parking area allows easy access to the tree farm from Leber Lane. From here, Dickerson Falls Trail enters the forest immediately before opening up to a wide powerline cut. Then it's right back into the woods again. Brace for a short yet steep climb through this section. Big cedar trees provide plenty of shade and shelter from the elements overhead. The trail continues gaining elevation as it rolls along—sometimes steeply, sometimes gently—between Dickerson Creek and a logging road. At 0.5 miles, we encountered a rope tied between trees along a particularly steep trail section, presumably to help hikers stay steady on the incline.

Dickerson Falls is the highlight of the public trail system on Ueland Tree Farm.

A canopy of green keeps the hike well shaded—and shows off the beauty of the tree farm.

After 0.8 miles of wooded walking, you'll pop out onto a gravel road. Head right for the falls, encountering a signed junction in another 0.3 miles. Soon you'll cross a volunteer-built bridge, constructed in 2017 by members of the Evergreen Mountain Bike Alliance. Wood for the bridge was sourced from the tree farm and milled onsite. It's all downhill from here: the trail descends rapidly to the falls via steps and switchbacks. You'll reach the falls in no time, where a fallen tree provides perfect sit-and-selfie views of the falls. Visit during winter and spring—after periods of heavy rain—for the best viewing experience. We hiked here in late summer, when the falls were just a trickle, but still worth the minimal effort to reach them. Return the way you came.

Going Further: Several miles of trails follow the gravel roads through Ueland Tree Farm. Check the trailhead map for reference, or download a map on your phone from the tree farm's website (see link above). Try the 3-mile roundtrip South Loop Trail to follow logging roads through Douglas Fir forest and wetlands. Or hike all the way to Zach's Lookout, a 6.5-mile roundtrip trek from the trailhead. From this 1,040-foot perch, you can enjoy views across Hood Canal to the Olympic Mountains.

MILES AND DIRECTIONS

0.0   Begin from the signed trailhead at the west end of the parking lot, walking west on the Dickerson Falls Trail. Stay on the dirt trail at all road junctions.

0.8   Turn right onto the gravel road.

1.1   Turn right at the Dickerson Creek Waterfall sign.

1.2   Reach the falls. Turn around here and retrace your steps to the trailhead.

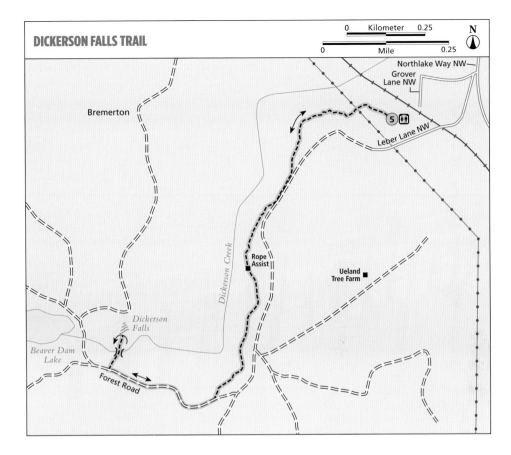

Bremerton

Northlake Way NW—
Grover
Lane NW

Leber Lane NW

5

Dickerson Creek

Rope
Assist

Ueland
Tree Farm

Dickerson
Falls

Beaver Dam
Lake

Forest Road

LOCAL INTEREST

Silver City Brewery Taproom: A quick 3 miles down the road from Ueland Tree Farm, this classic Kitsap County brewery has been serving the community since 1996. Beer-focused, 21+ taproom. Address: 206 Katy Penman Ave., Bremerton, WA; Phone: (360) 813-1487; Web: www.silvercity.beer/taproom

LODGING

Flagship Inn: Reasonably priced waterfront motel overlooking Oyster Bay, located just 3 miles from the trailhead. Relax with balcony views and a continental breakfast. Address: 4320 Kitsap Way, Bremerton, WA; Phone: (360) 479-6566; Web: www.flagshipinn.com

A jogger on Taylor Dock heading to Fairhaven.

NORTHWEST WASHINGTON

North of Seattle and west of the Cascade Mountains, Northwest Washington includes the bayside city of Bellingham, the fertile Skagit Valley, and the island gateway city of Anacortes. With easy access to forested trails, saltwater shoreline, and freshwater lakes and creeks, it's all about the abundant woods and water in these parts.

Perched over Bellingham Bay, the college town of Bellingham is an outdoor lover's playground surrounded by mountains, evergreen forest, and the Salish Sea. Bellingham's proximity to the US-Canadian border—between the international cities of Seattle and Vancouver, BC—makes it an ideal stopover for regional road-trippers. Experience Bellingham's natural beauty on the South Bay Trail between downtown and historic Fairhaven—a bayside walk through the city's most beloved park. In forested city parks east of I-5, Lake Padden and Whatcom Falls are local hotspots for urban outings.

The Skagit Valley's bays and beaches beckon urban explorers of all ages. Venture to an eelgrass estuary where the Wild and Scenic Skagit River meets the bay after its 150-mile journey from the Canadian Cascades. At the flat, kid friendly Padilla Bay Shore Trail, the landscape changes with the tides. Home to wintering snow geese, great blue herons, and soaring bald eagles, this urban hike is a birder's dream.

Separated from the mainland by the Swinomish Channel, Fidalgo Island is accessed via twin bridges. At the island's northern end is the city of Anacortes, whose ferry port is the jumping-off point to the spectacular San Juan Islands. But you don't have to board a ferry to enjoy the seaside scenery. Watch the ferries come and go from Anacortes's Guemes Channel Trail with the islands as their backdrop. At Fidalgo Island's southern end you'll find Deception Pass. Traversed by the 180-foot high Deception Pass Bridge, this swirling strait is the namesake for Washington's most-visited state park. View the bridge from the beach and look down on the waters from seaside cliffs in this unique marine environment.

6 LAKE PADDEN LOOP

Walk the easy 2.8-mile loop around Lake Padden for access to both leisure and recreation on the outskirts of Bellingham. This beloved park is a family favorite.

Elevation gain: 150 feet
Distance: 2.8-mile loop
Hiking time: 1–2 hours
Difficulty: Easy
Seasons: Year round
Trail surface: Gravel path, paved path
Land status: City park
Nearest town: Bellingham
Other users: Joggers, cyclists, equestrians
Water availability: Yes, at restrooms

Canine compatibility: Dogs must remain on leash along the main loop. An off-leash dog park and trails are available.
Fees and permits: None
Map: Lake Padden Park Trail Map - City of Bellingham Parks: www.cob .org/services/recreation/parks-trails/ Pages/lake-padden-park.aspx
Trail contact: City of Bellingham Parks: (360) 778-7000
Trailhead GPS: N48.7057 W122.4563

FINDING THE TRAILHEAD

From Bellingham, take I-5 south to exit 252 for Samish Way. Turn left onto S Samish Way, then turn right to stay on S Samish Way. Drive 2.1 miles to the signed West Lake Padden parking lot on the right. Park near the restrooms.

WHAT TO SEE

Located a few miles outside of downtown Bellingham, Lake Padden is a local treasure. College students, families, and everyone in between enjoy sprawling out on the lake's grassy lawns for lakeside BBQs, sunbathing, swimming, and paddling. A 2.8-mile loop trail encircles the lake, making for an easy 1-hour walk any time of year. And because the lake is only open to nonmotorized watercraft, you can experience some peace and quiet along the way. Close to town yet full of natural scenery, this is one urban trail that checks all the boxes—earning a place among our favorite Bellingham urban trails.

Begin your hike from the beach along Lake Padden's north shore. Walking east for a clockwise loop, you'll pass between cottonwood and conifer forest with views across the lake. Picnic tables—some with barbecues—are spread throughout the park, making it one of Bellingham's favorite places for a sunset barbeque during warmer months. Road noise is noticeable along this northern stretch, but soon it dissipates as you round the lake to its darker, quieter south side.

After passing the boat launch and a dock (more summer hotspots), you'll arrive at Lake Padden's busy recreation area. Picnic shelters, a large playground, and basketball court give way to the ball fields and dog park on this happening stretch. Ducks can often be found napping and waddling along the lakeshore here. This first mile is mostly flat and easy, with exposed lake views and little protection from the elements. Once you reach the southeast end of the lake, the trail makes a hairpin turn into the deep, dark forest and begins to climb.

Trek through dense forest along this rolling stretch, coming to a pair of carved benches at 2.0 miles. Though the grade is never very steep, you'll gain over 100 feet of elevation

The fishing dock gives an expansive view of Lake Padden and is a popular spot for swimming in the summer.

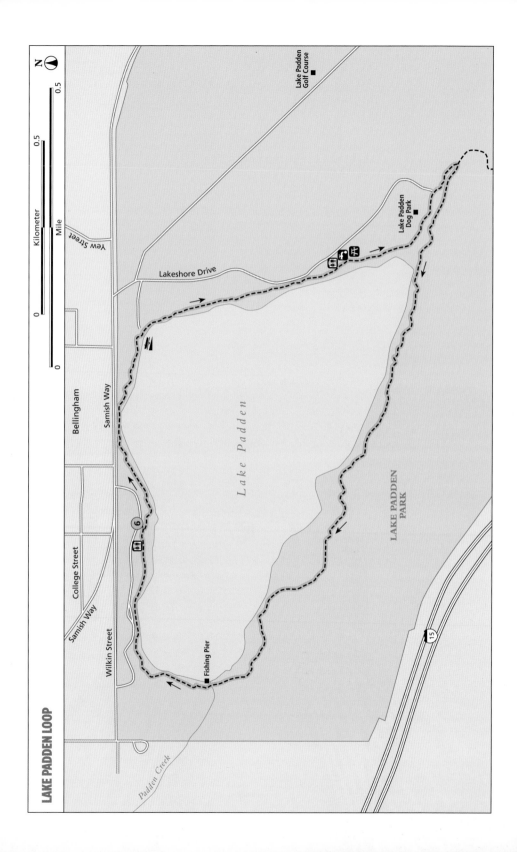

LAKE PADDEN LOOP

N

Kilometer
0   0.5
Mile
0   0.5

Yew Street

Lakeshore Drive

Bellingham

Samish Way

College Street

Samish Way

Wilkin Street

Fishing Pier

6

Lake Padden

LAKE PADDEN
PARK

Lake Padden
Dog Park

Lake Padden
Golf Course

Padden Creek

15

before finishing the loop. Horse trails radiate south from the loop trail, making several steeper loops for those seeking a workout. At 2.4 miles reach the lake's outlet at Padden Creek, where the Padden Gorge Trail takes off west. Stay to the right on the main loop here, but be sure to pause at the fishing dock for the lake's best viewpoint. Peering east across the waters, you'll see Lookout Mountain rising above pristine Lake Padden. Continue along the loop to reach the trailhead parking lot at 2.8 miles.

Going Further: From the off-leash dog trail junction at 1.1 miles, you can head east on either of the two paths for a few fun loop options. Dogs can roam free east of the Padden Creek crossing. You can also explore the horse trails on the south side of the lake. Or head west along the Padden Gorge Trail for 0.5 miles to 36th Street, where a short lollipop loop option is available. Most major trail intersections are signed with a map, but it's helpful to bring your own trail map if departing from the main loop.

MILES AND DIRECTIONS

0.0   From the trailhead near the restrooms, begin by walking east on the gravel loop trail. Stay on this main trail (stick to the water) at all trail intersections.

1.1   Reach a junction with the off-leash dog trails. Stay to the right for the main loop.

2.8   Arrive back at the restrooms and trailhead.

LOCAL INTEREST

Lake Padden Golf Course: Fancy a round of golf? This eighteen-hole course has you covered, with a full-service restaurant on site. Address: 4882 Samish Way, Bellingham, WA; Phone: (360) 738-7400; Web: www.lakepaddengolf.com

LODGING

Hotel Leo: Stylish downtown digs in the historic Leopold Hotel, originally built in 1883 and restored in 2019. Address: 1224 Cornwall Ave., Bellingham, WA; Phone: (360) 733-3500; Web: www.thehotelleo.com

7 SOUTH BAY TRAIL

The South Bay Trail connects Fairhaven Historic District to the heart of downtown Bellingham. A showcase tour of the city's charms, this waterfront walkway is a local favorite highlighting Bellingham's natural beauty. If you only have one day to spend outdoors in Bellingham, spend it here.

Elevation gain: 100 feet
Distance: 5.0 miles out-and-back
Hiking time: 2 hours
Difficulty: Easy
Seasons: Year round
Trail surface: Paved path, gravel, boardwalk
Land status: City park
Nearest town: Bellingham
Other users: Cyclists, joggers
Water availability: Yes, at restrooms

Canine compatibility: Dogs must remain on leash
Fees and permits: None
Map: South Bay Trail and Boulevard Park - City of Bellingham Parks
Trail contact: City of Bellingham Parks and Recreation: (360) 778-7000
Trailhead GPS: N48°43.259' W122°30.269'

FINDING THE TRAILHEAD

From Exit 250 on I-5, follow Old Fairhaven Parkway west for 1.3 miles. Turn right onto 14th Street. Drive 0.2 mile, then turn left onto Harris Avenue. Drive 0.2 mile, then turn right onto 11th Street. Park in the large gravel lot on the left. Additional free parking is available throughout Fairhaven, though some spots have a 2-hour limit. The trailhead is located above the southeast corner of the parking lot and can be accessed at the intersection of Mill Avenue and 10th Street.

WHAT TO SEE

It's worth exploring Fairhaven's well preserved, brick-building shops and restaurants before embarking on this urban hike. Located across from Fairhaven Village Green, the South Bay Trail starts at the corner of Mill Ave and 10th Street on a well-maintained wide gravel path. For the first 0.3 mile, the trail passes behind the businesses of Fairhaven, overlooking the Bellingham Ferry Terminal through overgrown brambles of blackberries.

You'll soon come to a parking area off 10th Street. Stay to the west side of the street and arrive at a paved terrace with a stunning viewpoint and public restrooms. Fill up a water bottle here, and pause to take in the view of Bellingham Bay. This is the entrance to Taylor Dock, arguably the highlight of the South Bay Trail. A remnant of industrial waterfront, Taylor Dock was restored in 2004. You'll likely pass families, joggers, and cyclists out enjoying the sea air. Arguably the best trail in town for a sunset stroll, there are plenty of benches along the way to take in the views. To the south, the Chuckanut Range climbs above Fairhaven. Looking west you'll spot Lummi Island across the bay, and on clear days the Canadian Coast Mountains are visible to the north. On crisp winter days, Golden Ears' twin peaks are easy to spot with their snowy caps.

At 0.8 mile, you'll reach Boulevard Park, another popular destination for Bellinghamsters to stretch their legs. In the summer, the park hosts an outdoor concert series in the bandstand at the north end of the park, and the lawn is prime real estate for Fourth

of July fireworks viewing. But no matter what season, if the sun is out you're likely to see college students taking a study break, and kids playing along the newly reclaimed shoreline.

Keep west at the coffee shop to continue on the pedestrian path along Boulevard Park's shoreline. Follow the paved walkway past a busy seafaring-themed playground and the stage before veering inland near the northern restrooms. Here, another small beach is nestled between train track and trail. Follow the trail across the railroad tracks to head north on a mile-long, uninterrupted gravel section of the South Bay Trail.

Along the way, several staircases lead up to State Street on your right, while peek-a-boo bay views are visible through the trees to your left. Interpretive signs elaborate on Bellingham history, with a monument marking the former boundary between the towns of Fairhaven and Whatcom. You can also read up on Rail Trail Historic Sites thanks to signposts provided by the Bellingham Railway Museum. Bellingham's industrial water-front is undergoing redevelopment and will one day host another waterfront park.

Look across the industrial park below to spot a massive mountain mural on one of the warehouses. Painted by Bellingham artist Gretchen Leggitt in 2018, the mural covers 22,000 square feet of wall space—the largest mural in the state of Washington. Soon you'll cross Wharf Street onto an old trestle before entering a residential and commercial area at the edge of downtown Bellingham. The trail ends somewhat abruptly at a trail-head sign on East Laurel Street. But it's worth continuing down to Railroad Avenue a short distance to reach Depot Market Square: the heart of downtown. Here, the Bellingham Farmers Market is bustling on Saturdays. Several breweries and eateries are within walking distance. When you've had your fill, turn around here and retrace your steps to Fairhaven.

Taylor Dock extends over Bellingham Bay.

MILES AND DIRECTIONS

0.0 Start at the South Bay Trailhead, across the street from Fairhaven Village Green. Head north on the trail towards downtown Bellingham.

0.2 Meet up with 10th Street. Keep to west side of the road.

0.3 Arrive at the terrace entrance to Taylor Dock. Turn left to enter Taylor Dock.

0.4 When the dock levels out, turn right to follow the boardwalk towards Boulevard Park.

0.6 Once you reach the end of Taylor Dock, continue straight to connect to Pattle Point Trestle.

0.8 Arrive at Boulevard Park and keep left to continue on the paved pedestrian path to the west of the coffee shop.

1.1 After the path curves, turn left across a pedestrian railway crossing. Keep left to stay on the South Bay Trail.

2.2 Cross Wharf Street and continue onto the trestle. Continue straight through the alley.

2.4 Turn left at the trailhead sign on East Laurel St., follow the sidewalk as it curves to the left and meets up with Railroad Avenue alley.

2.5 Cross Maple Street to arrive at the "Goatcart" statue outside of Depot Market Square. This is your turnaround point.

5.0 Arrive back at the trailhead in Fairhaven.

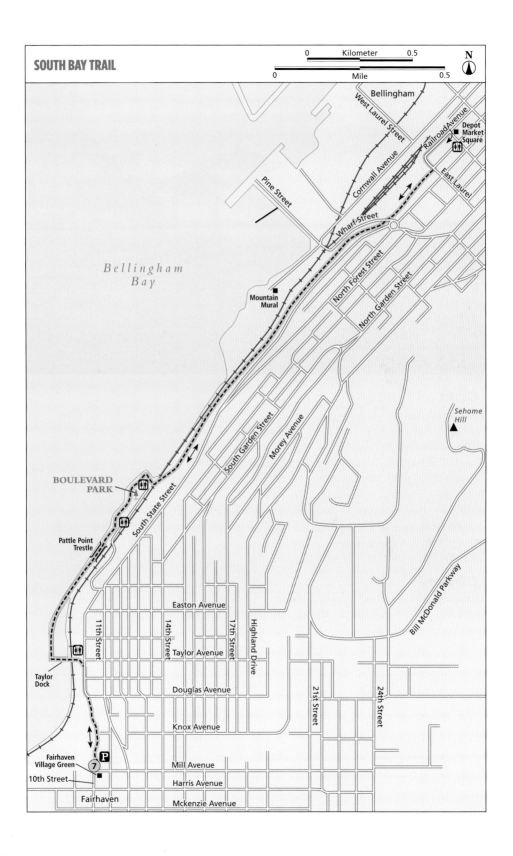

SOUTH BAY TRAIL

N

0   Kilometer   0.5
0   Mile   0.5

Bellingham

West Laurel Street

Cornwall Avenue

Railroad Avenue

Depot
Market
Square

East Laurel

Pine Street

Wharf Street

Bellingham
Bay

North Forest Street

North Garden Street

Mountain
Mural

Sehome
Hill

South Garden Street

Morey Avenue

BOULEVARD
PARK

South State Street

Pattle Point
Trestle

Bill McDonald Parkway

Easton Avenue

11th Street

14th Street

17th Street

Highland Drive

Taylor Avenue

21st Street

24th Street

Taylor
Dock

Douglas Avenue

Knox Avenue

Fairhaven
Village Green

P

7

10th Street

Mill Avenue

Harris Avenue

Fairhaven

Mckenzie Avenue

Boulevard Park's bandstand hosts a summer concert series.

LOCAL INTEREST

Village Books: Browse for books or grab coffee and sweets upstairs at Fairhaven's finest bookstore. Address: 1200 11th St., Bellingham, WA; Phone: (360) 671-2626; Web: www.villagebooks.com

Woods Coffee: The Woods's Boulevard Park location makes for a convenient (and scenic) stop along the South Bay Trail. Address: 470 Bayview Dr, Bellingham, WA; Phone: (360) 738-4771; Web: www.woodscoffee.com

Boundary Bay Brewery: The oldest brewpub in Bellingham has been serving pints and pub grub since 1995. Address: 1107 Railroad Trail, Bellingham, WA; Phone: (360) 647-5593; Web: www.bbaybrewery.com

LODGING

Fairhaven Village Inn: Boutique twenty-two-room inn located just steps from the South Bay Trail. Address: 1200 10th St., Bellingham, WA; Phone: (360) 733-1311; Web: www.fairhavenvillageinn.com

8 WHATCOM CREEK TRAIL

Follow Whatcom Creek to experience waterfalls, lakeside views, and railway history—all in just two miles of walking.

> **Elevation gain:** 150 feet
> **Distance:** 2.1-mile circuit
> **Hiking time:** 1-2 hours
> **Difficulty:** Easy
> **Seasons:** Year round
> **Trail surface:** Dirt, gravel, paved path
> **Land status:** City park
> **Nearest town:** Bellingham
> **Other users:** Cyclists, joggers
> **Water availability:** Yes, at restrooms
>
> **Canine compatibility:** On-leash and off-leash areas
> **Fees and permits:** None
> **Map:** Whatcom Falls Trail Map - City of Bellingham Parks
> **Trail contact:** City of Bellingham Parks and Recreation: (360) 778-7000
> **Trailhead GPS:** N48°45.075' W122°25.735'

FINDING THE TRAILHEAD

 From Exit 253 on 1-5, head east on Lakeway Drive for 1.4 miles. Turn left onto Silver Beach Road at the entrance to Whatcom Falls Park. Drive 0.4 mile. Parking spaces are available on both sides of the road, and the signed trailhead is on the west side of the parking lot.

WHAT TO SEE

From the massive spray of Snoqualmie Falls to the rivulets of alpine waters that give the Cascade Mountains their name, Washington has its share of notable waterfalls. Bellingham's Whatcom Falls Park is home to a set of namesake cascades, which create a forested oasis of babbling waters and historic landmarks—all a hop, skip, and a jump from the downtown core.

Begin your hike at Whatcom Falls Park, whose lush forest canopy provides shelter from the elements. Follow the paved trail as it descends gently to a grand Stone Bridge, built between 1939-1940 by Works Progress Administration (WPA) crews. Constructed from salvaged Chuckanut sandstone, the bridge's materials once formed the arches of a downtown building. Halfway across the bridge, you'll find yourself face-to-face with Whatcom Falls. Though not particularly tall, the falls can swell to some 40 feet wide during rainier months. Take a moment here to look and listen. A native word meaning "noisy water," Whatcom is the perfect name for Bellingham's favorite waterfall. Visit during winter for the best flows.

From the far end of the bridge, trails take off in three different directions. Optional excursions include a trail to Whirlpool Falls, a popular summer swimming hole. Hang a right to follow Whatcom Creek north to its source. Along the way, you'll pass some smaller falls before climbing a 60-foot staircase up to the Whatcom Creek Greenway. Cross Whatcom Creek again via bridge, then cross Electric Avenue to transition from forest to open field. The multipurpose fields at Bloedel Donovan Park are designated dog off-leash areas during posted hours (6 a.m. to 10 a.m. daily). Dogs must remain on-leash at all other times.

Continue across the parking lot to the Lake Whatcom waterfront. The surrounding shoreline is mostly residential, making Bloedel Donovan Park a special place for public

Whatcom Falls as seen from Stone Bridge in summer.

access. Take advantage of the tables and BBQ grills if you've packed a picnic, or simply sit and enjoy views of the enormous Lake Whatcom. Geese and ducks make regular appearances. The beach is a popular swimming spot during summertime, and a playground provides fun for kids year round.

When you've had your fill of lake time, retrace your steps to the Railroad Trail Bridge over Whatcom Creek. Stay left here to loop back to the parking lot. Along the way, you'll pass beneath the skeleton of a century-old train trestle. Built in 1916, it once linked Lake Whatcom's Larson Mill to Bellingham Bay. Imagine trains chugging overhead as you pass beneath the towering structure. Cut from the shores of Lake Whatcom, timber was floated to the mill and transferred by train to the bay.

Continue on the path between Whatcom Creek and residential backyards before arriving at Derby Pond. Open seasonally for youth fishing (ages 14 and under), this pond is stocked by the nearby fish hatchery. Take a seat at one of the benches and watch the ducks go by. Derby Pond's tranquil setting offers a nice contrast to the noisy waters of Whatcom Falls—a peaceful way to end your walk.

MILES AND DIRECTIONS

0.0 Begin by walking west down the signed trail to Whatcom Falls.

0.1 After crossing the Stone Bridge, turn right at the signed junction to head north towards Bloedel Donovan Park.

0.3 Ascend the stairs, then turn right onto the Whatcom Creek Greenway. Continue straight on this trail for 0.3 miles.

0.6 Turn right on the Railroad Trail.

Ducks enjoying a swim at Derby Pond.

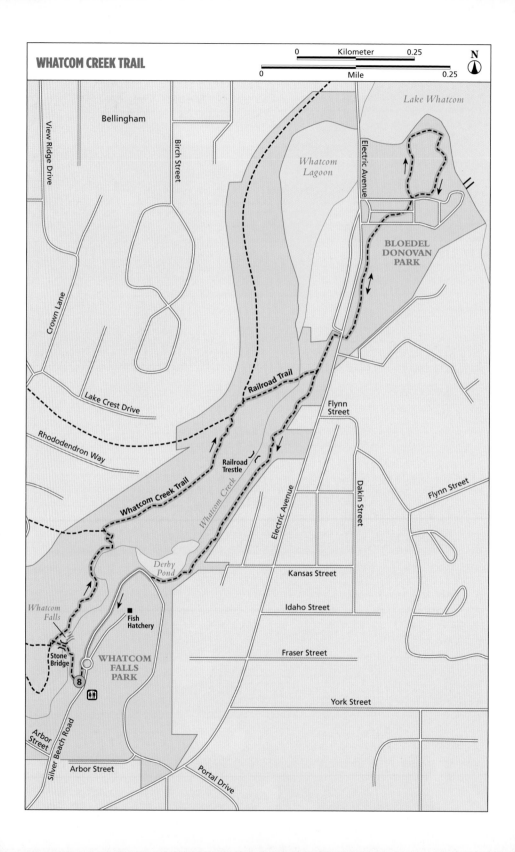

WHATCOM CREEK TRAIL

Kilometer 0 0.25

Mile 0 0.25

N

Lake Whatcom

Bellingham

View Ridge Drive

Birch Street

Whatcom Lagoon

Electric Avenue

BLOEDEL DONOVAN PARK

Crown Lane

Railroad Trail

Lake Crest Drive

Flynn Street

Rhododendron Way

Railroad Trestle

Flynn Street

Whatcom Creek Trail

Whatcom Creek

Electric Avenue

Dakin Street

Derby Pond

Kansas Street

Idaho Street

Whatcom Falls

Fish Hatchery

Stone Bridge

WHATCOM FALLS PARK

Fraser Street

8

Arbor Street

Silver Beach Road

York Street

Arbor Street

Portal Drive

A snowy salmon bench at Derby Pond.

0.7	Cross the Railroad Trail bridge, then turn left. Follow the Railroad Trail as it crosses Electric Avenue at 0.8 miles.
0.8	After crossing Electric Avenue, continue north on the Railroad Trail.
1.0	Cross the parking lot and continue north into Bloedel Donovan Park.
1.2	Explore the shoreline, then head south and return to the Railroad Trail at 1.4 miles.
1.6	At the Railroad Trail Bridge junction, continue south (left).
1.7	Reach the trestle and continue straight.
2.0	Reach Derby Pond. Turn left at the salmon bench to follow Silver Beach Road back to the parking lot.

LOCAL INTEREST

Lafeens Family Pride Donuts and Ice Cream: Located across Electric Avenue from the park, Lafeens is a longtime family favorite for sweets. Address: 1466 Electric Ave. Bellingham, WA; Phone: (360) 647-1703; Web: www.facebook.com/LafeensFamilyPride Donuts

Kulshan Brewing: Kulshan's Kentucky Street location is a convenient stop for post-hike beers in the nearby Roosevelt neighborhood. Address: 1538 Kentucky St., Bellingham, WA; Phone: (360) 389-5348; Web: www.kulshanbrewing.com

LODGING

Chrysalis Inn & Spa: This lovely waterfront hotel overlooks Taylor Dock and Bellingham Bay. Address: 804 10th St., Bellingham, WA; Phone: (360) 756-1005; Web: www.thechrysalisinn.com

9 GUEMES CHANNEL - SHIP HARBOR TRAILS

Two flat shoreline trails trace the edge of Guemes Channel and Ship Harbor for family friendly beach and seaview access. Sunsets here are spectacular.

Elevation gain: Minimal
Distance: 2.8 miles out and back
Hiking time: 1-2 hours
Difficulty: Easy
Seasons: Year round
Trail surface: Paved path, gravel, boardwalk
Land status: City park
Nearest town: Anacortes
Other users: Joggers

Water availability: None available
Canine compatibility: Dogs must remain on leash
Fees and permits: None
Map: Guemes Channel Trail - Anacortes Parks Foundation
Trail contact: Anacortes Parks Foundation: (360) 293-1918
Trailhead GPS: N48°30.230' W122°40.224'

FINDING THE TRAILHEAD

From Exit 230 on I-5, take WA-20 West for 11.3 miles. Stay right at the spur to continue to Anacortes. After 2.6 miles, take the first exit onto Commercial Avenue. Drive 1.3 miles, then turn left onto 12th Street. Drive 1.1 miles and continue straight onto Oakes Avenue. After 1.6 miles, turn right onto Ship Harbor Boulevard. Drive 300 feet, then turn left onto Edwards Way. Park in the cul-de-sac at the end of the road.

WHAT TO SEE

The Guemes Channel Trail and Ship Harbor Trail are vital links in a chain of paths connecting Fidalgo Island's northern shoreline. Eventually, these links will connect Washington Park and the San Juan Ferry to the Tommy Thompson Trail—an ambitious trail-building project many miles and years in the making. For now, you can enjoy some of the most scenic sections of this Cross Island Connection at Guemes Channel and Ship Harbor. Bring the stroller and the whole family—these easy-to-access trails are great for all ages and abilities.

From the cul-de-sac parking lot, you'll immediately be rewarded with views of Cypress Island and the surrounding San Juans. Listen for the ferry's boarding call and watch as ships come and go—you're less than a mile from the ferry dock and about to get even closer. An interpretive sign at the trailhead explains how this historic fishing site came to be known as Ship Harbor in the mid-1850s. When you're ready, set out west on the compressed gravel Ship Harbor Trail for beach access and boardwalks at the interpretive preserve.

You'll gain beach access in no time. Walk out onto the sandy shoreline during low tide to discover marine wildlife and listen to the sounds of the Salish Sea. Interpretive signs along the trail describe its native flora and fauna, while wooden platforms and benches provide various viewpoints. When you come to the cormorant statue, look out for these large birds perched on pilings, drying their wings in the sun.

Big leaf maple trees provide a colorful canopy in the fall on the Guemes Channel Trail.

Soon you'll come to the Ship Harbor Trail boardwalk. The 6-foot-wide wooden walkway provides wetland access via a small loop. It also continues west at a junction towards the Washington State Ferry terminal—an optional side trip for access to restrooms and services. For those waiting in the ferry line, a walk along the Ship Harbor Trail is a fun and refreshing way to pass the time. Listen for the throaty trill of the red-winged blackbird as you walk through the wetlands, then return to the main trail and head back to the parking lot.

After completing the 0.7-mile Ship Harbor Trail lollipop, head northeast on the Guemes Channel Trail. This section of trail extends 1.1 miles from the cul-de-sac to Lovric's Marina. This paved path is quite different from Ship Harbor Trail, raised slightly to form a seawall and guarded on the south side by overhanging trees. Peer past the wooden fence line and tall grass to sea views and Mount Baker. Erosion on the south side of the trail is visible in places, causing the Guemes Channel Trail to occasionally close due to mudslides. Near the end of the trail, a steep staircase leads up to tiny Roadside Park—an alternate entry point to the trail.

The end of the Guemes Channel Trail is clearly marked by a fence and signage. From here you can spot La Merced—a schooner-turned-breakwater at Lovric's Marina. Due to its visibility from the road, many passerby have wondered at the history of this "shipwreck." Turns out, it's no shipwreck at all. Filled with sand, the old schooner has been reclaimed by Mother Nature in the form of trees sprouting from her hull. Read up on La Merced's history before returning the way you came.

GUEMES CHANNEL - SHIP HARBOR TRAILS

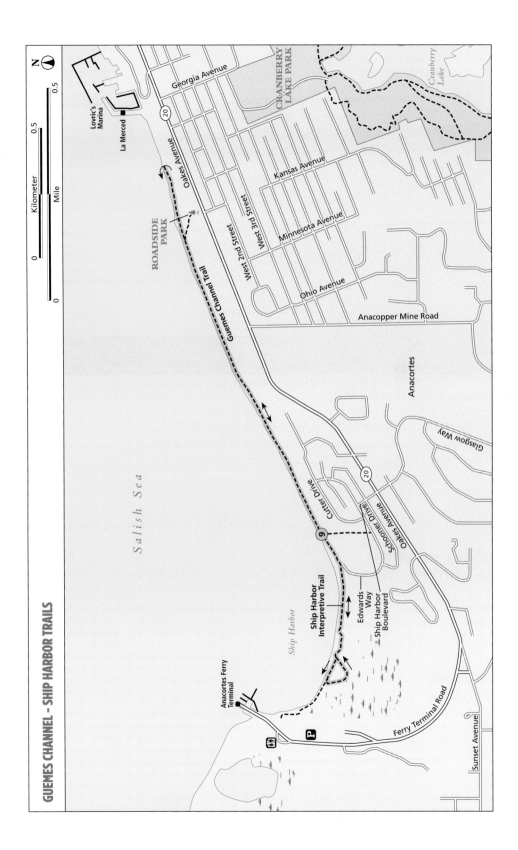

N

Kilometer
0   0.5   0.5

Mile
0

Lovric's Marina

La Merced

Georgia Avenue

CRANBERRY LAKE PARK

Cranberry Lake

20

Oakes Avenue

Kansas Avenue

ROADSIDE PARK

Minnesota Avenue

West 2nd Street

West 3rd Street

Guemes Channel Trail

Ohio Avenue

Anacopper Mine Road

Salish Sea

Anacortes

Glasgow Way

Cutter Drive

20

9

Schooner Drive

Oakes Avenue

Ship Harbor Interpretive Trail

Ship Harbor

Edwards Way

* Ship Harbor Boulevard

Anacortes Ferry Terminal

Ferry Terminal Road

Sunset Avenue

La Merced schooner and Mount Baker from the Guemes Channel Trail.

MILES AND DIRECTIONS

0.0 Begin by walking west on the Ship Harbor Trail.

0.2 Stay right at a junction.

0.3 Turn left to take the boardwalk loop over the wetlands. Then retrace your steps to the trailhead.

0.7 Back at the trailhead, continue east on the Guemes Channel Trail.

1.8 Turn around at the end of the trail. Retrace your steps to the trailhead.

LOCAL INTEREST

San Juan Islands: While you're near the ferry dock, consider taking a Washington State Ferry to the San Juan Islands for a day trip or overnight stay. www.visitsanjuans.com.

Washington Park: Nearby Washington Park offers an excellent trail network, camping, picnic areas, and public beaches. Address: 6300 Sunset Ave., Anacortes, WA; Phone: (360) 293-1918; Web: www.anacorteswa.gov.

LODGING

Majestic Inn & Spa: Centrally located in downtown Anacortes, the Majestic offers island views from the upper floors and its seasonal rooftop patio. Address: 419 Commercial Ave., Anacortes, WA; Phone: (360) 299-1400; Web: www.majesticinnandspa.com.

10 DECEPTION PASS HEADLANDS

Located on two islands connected by an iconic bridge, Deception Pass State Park is the most-visited state park in Washington. Explore the Fidalgo Island side for forest, sea, and bridge views from pebble-strewn beaches and headland heights.

Elevation gain: 560 feet
Distance: 3.7 mile double lollipop
Hiking time: 1.5 hours
Difficulty: Easy-Moderate
Seasons: Year round
Trail surface: Gravel, packed dirt
Land status: State park
Nearest town: Anacortes
Other users: Joggers
Water availability: At restrooms

Canine compatibility: Dogs must remain on leash
Fees and permits: Discover Pass
Map: Official Park Map - Deception Pass Park Foundation
Trail contact: Washington State Parks: (360) 675-3767
Trailhead GPS: N48°25.002' W122°39.067'

FINDING THE TRAILHEAD

From Exit 230 on I-5, take WA-20 West for 11.3 miles. At the traffic circle, take the second exit and stay on WA-20 West toward Oak Harbor. Continue 0.7 mile. At another traffic circle, take the second exit to stay on WA-20 West. Continue 4.4 miles, then turn right onto Rosario Road. Drive 200 feet, then turn left onto Bowman Bay Road. Continue 0.3 mile, then turn left for the Bowman Bay parking area.

WHAT TO SEE

It's a sunny day in Western Washington and you're looking for the perfect hike. Should you stay cool with a trek through evergreen forest? Or hit the beach and soak up the sun? No need to choose between the two—you can have it all at the Deception Pass Headlands. Part of Deception Pass State Park, these headlands offer an excellent trail network accessible year round. Hiking at Deception Pass State Park is a quintessential Washington experience for visitors and locals alike.

Begin at Bowman Bay for access to ample parking, restrooms, a playground, and picnic area. Views from the parking area are promising: a pier stretches westward into the bay, pointing to tiny islands and the headlands you'll soon explore. Walk south past the pier—taking a detour out to its end if you wish—before encountering a short but steep and rocky bluff climb. You'll gain just 50 feet of elevation here, but the trail seems to soar above the bay as you peer down on the pier below. Overhead, madrone trees reach out to sea. In only 0.3 miles the trail has transformed from open beach to sheltered bluff—a taste of what's to come.

Cross the tombolo between Bowman and Lottie Bays to access Lighthouse Point. A sandy beach on the Bowman Bay side makes for a family friendly snack stop. From here, the trail climbs to a junction near a burnt-out tree—always a fun photo opp. Head left to hike the loop clockwise. Another rocky beach at 0.7 mile provides good views of the Deception Pass Bridge (to get even closer to the bridge, take an optional side trip out to

Sea cliffs at Rosario Head.

Lottie Point). Continuing around the Lighthouse Point Loop, the trail transforms again from old growth forest to grassy balds and sea cliffs. Enjoy unobstructed westerly island views before closing the loop and returning to the parking area at Bowman Bay.

Walk north through Bowman Bay's grassy picnic areas to reach the Civilian Conservation Corps (CCC) Interpretive Center. This Depression-era bathhouse-turned-museum is open seasonally between mid-May and Labor Day. Stop in for a CCC history lesson before continuing your hike. The trail climbs 140 feet over Bowman Bay, then drops to sea level again at Sharpe Cove. Check out the tidal pools at Rosario Beach before continuing towards the entrance to Rosario Head. Here you'll meet the Maiden of Deception Pass, a carved cedar pole depicting an important Samish Indian Nation legend.

Beyond the Maiden of Deception Pass the trail comes to a junction. Head left for a clockwise loop and you'll be standing atop Rosario Head in no time, with sweeping San Juan Island views from the sheer cliffs. This may be the most photo-worthy place in the entire park (besides the bridge, of course). Take a lunch break here, enjoying full sun exposure and views to the Olympic Mountains on a clear day. Be sure to keep kids and dogs nearby, and don't approach the edge of the 60-foot sea cliffs. There's no railing to prevent falls into the kelp beds below. When you've had your fill of seaside splendor, return the way you came to Bowman Bay.

Going Further: Drive or walk across the 180-foot-high Deception Pass Bridge for dizzying views of the waters below. You can also hike to Lottie Point for a unique perspective of the bridge.

DECEPTION PASS HEADLANDS

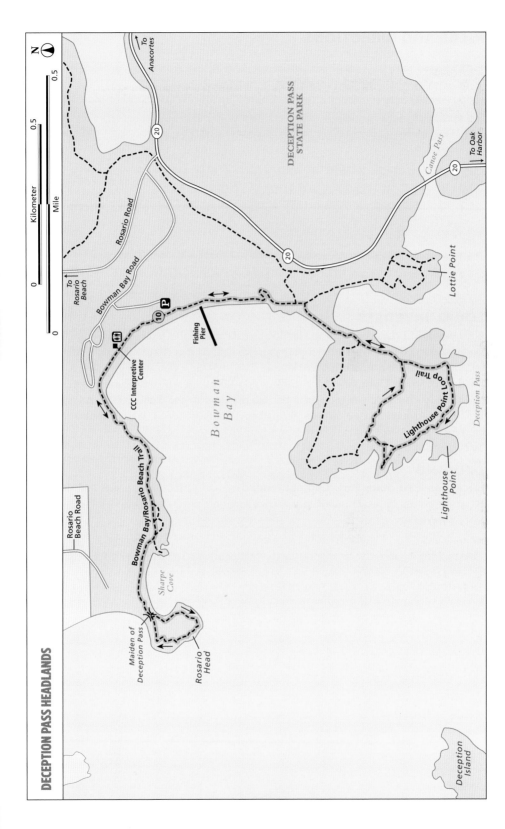

N

Kilometer
0   0.5
Mile
0   0.5

To Anacortes

20

Rosario Road

DECEPTION PASS STATE PARK

Canoe Pass

To Oak Harbor

20

20

Lottie Point

Bowman Bay Road

To Rosario Beach

P

10

Fishing Pier

CCC Interpretive Center

Rosario Beach Road

Bowman Bay

Bowman Bay/Rosario Beach Trail

Sharpe Cove

Loop Trail

Lighthouse Point Loop Trail

Deception Pass

Maiden of Deception Pass

Rosario Head

Lighthouse Point

Deception Island

MILES AND DIRECTIONS

0.0 Beginning by the boat launch, walk south along the beach trail.

0.3 At the Highway 20 trail junction, continue straight (south) towards Lighthouse Point. Then turn right at the Lottie Point trail junction for Lighthouse Point.

0.6 Stay left at the junction.

1.0 Turn left at the junction to reach a viewpoint. Then return to the Lighthouse Point Loop Trail.

1.1 Continue straight (east) at the junction.

1.3 Turn left to complete the loop and return to the parking area.

1.9 Back at the trailhead, walk north through the grassy picnic area and CCC Interpretive Center.

2.6 Stay left for Rosario Head.

2.7 Begin the Rosario Head loop by taking the trail to the left and heading south.

3.0 Complete the Rosario Head loop and return to the trailhead.

LOCAL INTEREST

GERE-a-DELI: Grab breakfast and locally roasted coffee before your adventure, or take sandwiches to go from Anacortes's favorite scratch deli. Always worth the wait. Address: 502 Commercial Ave, Anacortes, WA; Phone: (360) 293-7383; Web: www.gereadeli.com.

Bastion Brewing Company: Quench your post-hike thirst with a pint from the nearest brewpub. The family friendly taproom offers pub grub and daily specials. Address: 12529 Christianson Rd., Anacortes, WA; Phone: (360) 399-1614; Web: www.bastion brewery.com.

LODGING

Deception Pass State Park Campground: Tent and partial-hookup sites available. Reservations can be made online at www.washington.goingtocamp.com or by calling (888) 226-7688.

For additional lodging options in Anacortes, visit www.anacortes.org/stay.

11 PADILLA BAY SHORE TRAIL

Padilla Bay Shore Trail offers a flat and easy walk through the Padilla Bay National Estuarine Research Reserve, an eelgrass estuary excellent for birdwatching year round.

Elevation gain: 50 feet	**Water availability:** None
Distance: 4.8 miles out-and-back	**Canine compatibility:** Dogs must
Hiking time: 2 hours	remain on leash
Difficulty: Easy	**Fees and permits:** None
Seasons: Year round	**Map:** USGS La Conner
Trail surface: Packed gravel	**Trail contact:** Skagit County Parks:
Land status: County Park	(360) 416-1350
Nearest town: Burlington	**Trailhead GPS:** N48.4816 W122.4754
Other users: Joggers, cyclists	

FINDING THE TRAILHEAD

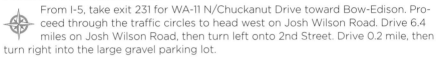

From I-5, take exit 231 for WA-11 N/Chuckanut Drive toward Bow-Edison. Proceed through the traffic circles to head west on Josh Wilson Road. Drive 6.4 miles on Josh Wilson Road, then turn left onto 2nd Street. Drive 0.2 mile, then turn right into the large gravel parking lot.

WHAT TO SEE

There are days for scaling mountains, and there are days for simply taking a walk. Padilla Bay is a place for the latter—a level, gravel shore trail meandering along a shallow bay. This gentle path winds along a dike constructed by early farmers in the Skagit Valley. Begin with a short stroll along Bayview Edison Road before turning south onto the shore trail. The skeleton of an old rowboat greets you trailside—a "shipwreck," perhaps, in the minds of curious kids. Families frequent the area on foot, bike, and with strollers, as Padilla Bay is the most kid friendly urban hike around.

You can see for miles and miles on a clear day. To the east, Mount Baker can be spotted rising high over the surrounding foothills. Westward, the views are of the San Juan Islands and Fidalgo Island. Across the bay, the Anacortes refinery at March Point blows smoke while Mount Erie rises beyond. Regardless of the weather, there's plenty to peer at in the surrounding estuary. At low tide, the bay becomes a mudflat full of crawly creatures—a feast for the various shorebirds who make this reserve their home.

Great blue herons hang out along the Padilla Bay Shore Trail, watching the waters for prey. Hundreds of these big birds have taken up residence across the bay at March Point, where a rookery on private Skagit Land Trust property provides shelter. 757 heron nests were counted in the area in 2018. The rookery is not open to the public, but you're likely to spot a heron or two during your Padilla Bay walk. To the east of the dike stretches the farmlands of Skagit Valley. In the winter months, these green fields play vacation home to snow geese and trumpeter swans. Bring binoculars for a closer look. Watch for bald eagles and other raptors here as well, especially during winter months.

Allow for around an hour or so of walking each way. The path snakes southward, as the dike crosses over sloughs with colorful names like "Big Indian" and "No Name" Slough.

The old barn is a favorite photo opportunity for hikers along Padilla Bay.

Expect a peaceful stroll, with plenty of benches to take a moment and breathe in the serenity. After 1.8 miles you'll reach an old barn, weathered grey, rusted tools sunken into the mud. The barn makes a great photo opp, but stay off of its unstable frame. Those who venture too far off-trail are liable to become a stick in the mud.

The trail ends abruptly at a small parking lot off Bayview Edison Road. Turn around here and retrace your steps, now taking in northern views. If you've timed your walk for sunset, you might enjoy a classic Pacific Northwest sunset over the bay on your way back to the car. Watch for alpenglow on Mount Baker as the sun slips beneath the horizon. On exceptionally clear days, you can even make out the outline of the Olympic Mountains in the distance—an adventure for another day.

MILES AND DIRECTIONS

0.0   From the parking lot, walk south (downhill) on 2nd Street to Bayview Edison Road.

0.1   Cross Bayview Edison Road and walk east along the shoulder. Turn right onto the Padilla Bay Shore Trail.

2.4   Reach the southern trailhead. Turn around here and retrace your steps.

LOCAL INTEREST

Breazeale Interpretive Center: This free-to-access (donations accepted) aquarium features fun educational exhibits for kids and adults alike. Address: 10441 Bayview Edison Rd., Mt Vernon, WA; Phone: (360) 428-1558; Web: www.ecology.wa.gov/Water -Shorelines/Shoreline-coastal-management/Padilla-Bay-reserve/

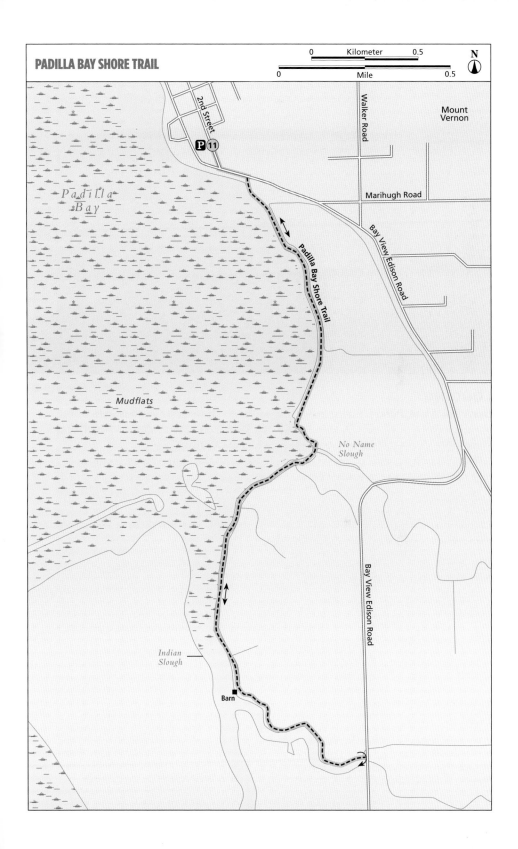

PADILLA BAY SHORE TRAIL

0   Kilometer   0.5

0   Mile   0.5

N

2nd Street

Walker Road

Mount Vernon

P 11

Marihugh Road

Padilla Bay

Bay View Edison Road

Padilla Bay Shore Trail

Mudflats

No Name Slough

Indian Slough

Barn

Bay View Edison Road

A heron walks along the estuary shore at sunset over Padilla Bay.

LODGING

Bay View State Park: This camping park on Padilla Bay is great for beachside BBQs, picnics, and overnight stays. Address: 10901 Bay View Edison Rd., Mount Vernon, WA; Phone: (360) 757-0227; Web: www.parks.state.wa.us/473/Bay-View

GREATER SEATTLE AREA

The Space Needle set against glacier-capped Mount Rainier: it's the image that has come to define Seattle. Washington State's largest and most populous city, Seattle is sandwiched between the waters of Puget Sound and Lake Washington. Spreading out from the banks of Lake Washington, cities and communities like Renton and Bellevue make up the urban core of the state. If you live near Lake Washington, you'll most likely tell people unfamiliar with Washington that you come from Seattle for the sake of simplicity.

The Greater Seattle Area is also home to some of Washington's most well-known companies, like Microsoft, Amazon, and Starbucks. The region is still growing, as new transplants move not just for industry, but increasingly because of the region's natural beauty. When city dwellers can't make it out to the Cascade Mountains for a taste of nature, they head to one of the many city parks in the region. From manicured gardens like Washington Park Arboretum to the sprawling wild spaces of Discovery Park, these green oases help hikers escape city traffic.

As urban sprawl continues, many of these green spaces are facing transitional periods. Renewed efforts to rehabilitate lakes, rivers, and forests mean that many of these parks are undergoing changes. Restoring shorelines and the natural flora of the area will hopefully promote healthier salmon populations—an integral part of the Puget Sound ecosystem.

Mount Rainier as seen through old pilings in Lake Washington.

Take a short (but steep) walk in the park to one of the most scenic beaches in Snohomish County for views across Puget Sound.

Elevation gain: 470 feet
Distance: 2.6 miles out-and-back
Hiking time: 1-2 hours
Difficulty: Moderate due to elevation gain
Seasons: Year round
Trail surface: Gravel and dirt path, paved path
Land status: County Park
Nearest town: Lynnwood
Other users: Joggers
Water availability: Yes, at picnic area

Canine compatibility: Dogs must remain on leash
Fees and permits: None
Map: Brochure—Meadowdale Beach - Snohomish County Parks: www .snohomishcountywa.gov/Facilities/ Facility/Details/Meadowdale-Beach-Park-56
Trail contact: Snohomish County Parks: (425) 388-6600
Trailhead GPS: N47.8572 W122.3162

FINDING THE TRAILHEAD

From I-5, take exit 183 for 164th Street SW. Follow 164th Street SW (signs for Alderwood Mall Parkway) west for 1.3 miles. Take a slight right to stay on 164th Street SW and continue for 0.7 mile. Turn right onto 52nd Avenue W, then drive 0.5 mile. Turn left onto 156th Street SW and continue for 0.6 mile to enter the park.

WHAT TO SEE

Surrounded by suburbia, Meadowdale Beach Park is so close, yet so far away from it all. Get a quick dose of forest-bathing, creekside splendor, and saltwater shoreline along this 1.3-mile urban trail—all packed into a county park that feels far more vast than its humble 108 acres. Incredibly, this park is hidden between Lynnwood and Everett just a few miles from Washington's busiest interstate highway. Thousands of cars zip by it every day, unaware of what they're missing. So next time you're stuck in Everett's notorious traffic on I-5 or Highway 99, consider Meadowdale for a welcome respite.

Head out on the wide path, spiraling down into dense forest. This trail drops from the get-go, making for a heart-pounding climb on the way back. After 0.3 mile of elevation loss, you'll come to a volunteer-built staircase. The stairs were constructed in 2017 by a Washington Trails Association work party, but the handrail—an Eagle Scout project— has been in place since 1994. After losing 300 feet of elevation in the first 0.4 mile, the trail mellows out and begins to parallel Lund's Gulch Creek.

Named after 1878-homesteader John Lund, the creek is home to both freshwater fish and migrating salmon. See if you can spot any, especially in the fall when salmon are running. Lund's Gulch Creek provides the soundtrack to your urban hike, while nurse stumps (left behind from old-growth Western redcedar), big leaf maple trees, and an array of greenery offer up visuals. Restful benches line the path—a detail you're more likely to notice on the return trip.

Once you reach the junction at 1.0 miles, head left for a clockwise loop. Pass the ranger's residence and Little Free Library before continuing to a picnic area on the vast lawn.

Restrooms and water are available here. When you're ready to hit the beach, continue beneath the train tracks through a low-pass pedestrian tunnel. Watch your head—and your feet. Lund's Gulch Creek empties into Puget Sound here, sometimes flooding the tunnel during winter. Bring waterproof boots if visiting during wetter months. Snohomish County Parks plans to restore the estuary in this area by removing the culvert and replacing it with a railroad bridge. Construction is planned for 2020–2021 and may impact access to the area. Check with Snohomish County Parks for current conditions.

At the end of the tunnel (or future bridge), views open up across Puget Sound to the Kitsap Peninsula, Whidbey Island, and the distant Olympic Mountains. Walk the rocky beach in either direction at low tide, find a driftwood bench, and watch the ferries on the water. This idyllic beach offers some of the wildest public coastline in the county—an urban oasis surrounded by the cities of Lynnwood, Edmonds, and Everett. Consider watching the sunset here, but don't linger too long: the beach closes 30 minutes before dusk, and the park gate is closed at dusk each evening. Enjoy the scenery, then make a short loop back to the main trail and return the way you came.

MILES AND DIRECTIONS

0.0 Begin from the east end of the parking lot at the trailhead kiosk. Walk south on the wide trail.

1.0 Turn left at the junction to pass the ranger residence and picnic area.

1.2 Turn left to enter the tunnel beneath the train tracks and reach the beach. Explore the beach, then return to this junction and turn left to make a short loop.

1.5 Continue straight on the trail, retracing your steps to the trailhead.

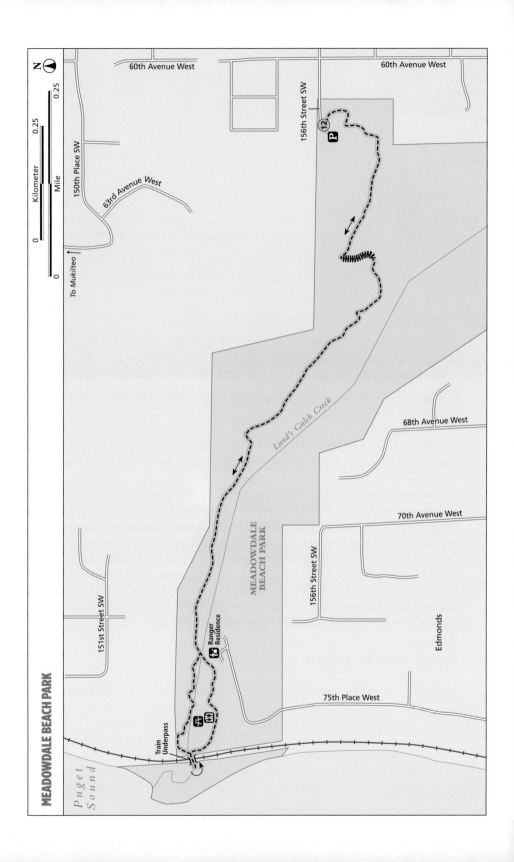

MEADOWDALE BEACH PARK

60th Avenue West

60th Avenue West

156th Street SW

150th Place SW

63rd Avenue West

12 P

To Mukilteo

Kilometer

0   0.25

0   0.25
Mile

N

Lund's Gulch Creek

68th Avenue West

70th Avenue West

156th Street SW

MEADOWDALE
BEACH PARK

Edmonds

151st Street SW

Ranger
Residence

75th Place West

Train
Underpass

Puget
Sound

This steep staircase winds down along the edge of Lund's Gulch.

LOCAL INTEREST

Astoria Pizza & Pasta: Popular pizza joint just 2 miles from the trailhead. Address: 4629 168th St. SW, Lynnwood, WA; Phone: (425) 745-5777; Web: www.astoriapizzaand pasta.com

LODGING

Villa Rivarola: Airbnb-style homestay near downtown Edmonds and Meadowdale Beach Park. Address: 345 12th Place N, Edmonds, WA; Phone: (425) 205-8603; Web: www.villa-rivarola.business.site

13 NORTH CREEK PARK

Traverse a floating pontoon boardwalk through a bog wetland integral to the health of Snohomish County's North Creek Watershed.

Elevation gain: 50 feet
Distance: 2 miles out-and-back
Hiking time: 1 hour
Difficulty: Easy
Seasons: Year round
Trail surface: Boardwalk, dirt path
Land status: County park
Nearest town: Mill Creek
Other users: Hikers only (bikes prohibited)
Water availability: None

Canine compatibility: Dogs must remain on leash
Fees and permits: None
Map: North Creek Park and Water Retention Facility - Snohomish County Parks: www .snohomishcountywa.gov/Facilities/ Facility/Details/North-Creek-Park-and-Water-Retention-Fac-103
Trail contact: Snohomish County Parks: (425) 388-6608
Trailhead GPS: N47.8327 W122.2190

FINDING THE TRAILHEAD

From I-5, take exit 183 for 164th Street SW. Turn east onto 164th Street SW (signs for Mill Creek) and drive 1.8 miles. Turn right onto WA-527 South and drive 1.3 miles. Turn right onto 183rd Street SE and drive 0.5 mile. Then turn right into North Creek Park. Begin your hike at the trailhead near the restrooms.

WHAT TO SEE

The distant hum of Bothell–Everett Highway is broken by the call of a circling red-tailed hawk. The outlines of businesses and neighboring apartment complexes are obscured by wetland grasses. Surrounded by urban sprawl, the wetlands of North Creek Park are a slice of wildness in the city.

North Creek Park includes a popular playground and picnic area, but the highlight of this park is the floating boardwalk across the peat bog. In the 1890s the Bailey Family worked this section of land. They raised cattle, collected peat, and sold the pelts of animals living in the bog. Now, this 28-acre space is returning to its wild state, acting as a water retention pond for storm runoff in the developed North Creek watershed. With headlands in south Everett, North Creek runs over 12 miles through the towns of Mill Creek and Bothell before flowing into the Sammamish River.

Start out from the parking lot, skirting the edge of the picnic area to reach the boardwalk. A unique trail experience, the boardwalk is actually made up of interconnected pontoon-supported wooden docks. The path itself is incredibly straightforward, simply an out-and-back with two short viewpoint spurs. Watch your footing after heavy rains as the boardwalk can get slick! Visits in the rain can be their own adventure as well—during a particularly rainy visit we actually saw a beaver walking along the boardwalk. In fact, beavers in this wetland are constantly building new ponds, reshaping the landscape.

As you travel deeper into the wetlands, you may notice a change in surrounding flora. Reed canary grass and cattails grow tall. In the summer months forget-me-nots and invasive spotted jewelweed flower along the trail. As the trail nears the deeper sections of bog and the swift Nickel Creek runs underfoot, beaked sedge pops up amongst the

Traverse over a marsh and peat bog on this unique boardwalk.

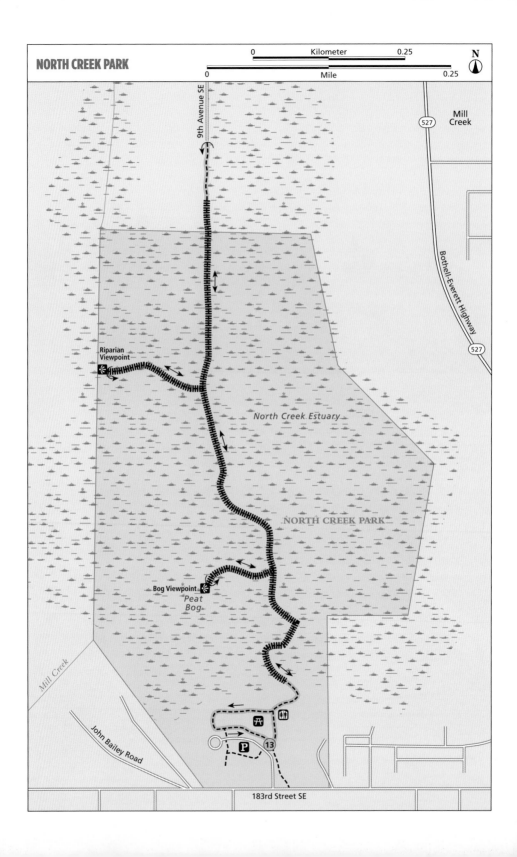

0   Kilometer   0.25

0   Mile   0.25

N

9th Avenue SE

527

Mill
Creek

Bothell-Everett Highway

527

Riparian
Viewpoint

North Creek Estuary

NORTH CREEK PARK

Bog Viewpoint
Peat
Bog

Mill Creek

John Bailey Road

P

13

183rd Street SE

other grasses. The tall grasses offer shelter to many animals, especially a number of birds. Listen for marsh wren and song sparrows—you might even spot the ebony flash of a redwing blackbird.

The first viewpoint offers you a chance to learn more about the peat bog. North Creek Park's peat bog is up to 20 feet thick in places, made of decaying plant matter. Part sponge, part filter, the peat bog absorbs stormwater runoff and also traps pollution deep in its acidic depths. This means that the water flowing into North Creek is cleaner, and severe flooding from storms is avoided. This place is more than just a park!

The second spur trail leads out to a view of the riparian zone along North Creek. Now mostly overgrown, the view is actually a window into the forested area along the creek. Cottonwoods and willow trees grow here, transitioning to Douglas spirea. Back on the main boardwalk, you'll soon cross the gurgling and rushing Nickel Creek. Undoubtedly you will hear them, but you should also be on the lookout for frogs. Since the boardwalk floats directly on the wetland waters, these amphibian friends can often be spotted sitting on the edge of the wood boards, their brown skin providing camouflage. Young hikers will enjoy an up-close look, but always remember to be respectful of the wildlife you encounter. This is their home you are visiting. After crossing the creek, you'll come to the end of the boardwalk and the northern reaches of North Creek Park. Turn around and head back the way you came to the parking lot, taking a detour through the picnic area if you wish.

MILES AND DIRECTIONS

0.0 Walk north on the main trail to reach the trailhead kiosk. Continue northeast from here.

0.2 Turn left at the Peat Bog Pond sign. Walk to the end of the spur, then retrace your steps to the sign and turn left (north) to continue.

0.6 Turn left at the Viewpoint sign. Walk to the end of the spur, then retrace your steps to the sign and turn left (north) to continue.

1.1 Reach the end of the trail. Turn around and retrace your steps to the trailhead kiosk.

1.8 Turn right after passing the kiosk to complete a short loop through the picnic area. Then return to the parking lot.

LOCAL INTEREST

Tablas Woodstone Taverna: A tapas bar with an excellent happy hour in downtown Mill Creek. Address: 15522 Main St., Mill Creek, WA; Phone: (425) 948-7654; Web: www.kafeneowoodstonegroup.com/tablas-woodstone-taverna/

LODGING

Extended Stay America: Hotel with rooms featuring kitchens and continental breakfast. Address: 3021 196th St. SW, Lynnwood, WA; Phone: (425) 670-2520; Web: www .extendedstayamerica.com/hotels/wa/seattle/lynnwood

14 SAMMAMISH RIVER TRAIL

Explore history along the City of Bothell's Sammamish River Trail to the newest and largest park in the city.

Elevation gain: 50 feet
Distance: 2.6-mile lollipop
Hiking time: 1–2 hours
Difficulty: Easy
Seasons: Year round
Trail surface: Paved path, gravel, grass
Land status: City park, county park
Nearest town: Bothell
Other users: Cyclists, joggers

Water availability: Yes, at restrooms
Canine compatibility: Dogs must remain on leash
Fees and permits: None
Map: Regional Trails in King County - King County Parks
Trail contact: King County Parks: (206) 296-0100
Trailhead GPS: N47°45.486', W122°12.504'

Finding the trailhead

From I-405, take exit 23 for WA-522 W. Drive 0.8 mile west on WA-522, then turn left onto NE 180th Street to access Bothell Landing Park. In 100 feet, turn right into the playground parking lot. Begin your walk from the southeast corner of the parking lot.

WHAT TO SEE

A town that once personified the word "quaint," Bothell is now experiencing a revitalization as the downtown core welcomes new businesses and restaurants and the city's population grows. From the Sammamish River Trail, you'll have a front-row seat to watch a city literally grow up, navigating the tenuous relationship between urbanization and the natural world.

Begin at Bothell Landing Park and explore a slice of history. The park's facilities include a playground, kayak rental facilities, an amphitheater, and a collection of historic Bothell structures. Home to the Bothell Historic Museum, stop in on Sundays, April-October to learn about Bothell's past. You can also walk around the outside of the three historic buildings, including the Hannan House (1893), the first Bothell Schoolhouse (1885), and the Beckstrom Log Cabin (1884).

From the east end of the park, cross the Sammamish River over a wooden bridge to meet up with the Sammamish River Trail, and turn right. The paved route is bicycle friendly, but the majority of cyclists take to the nearby Burke-Gilman Trail instead. The stroll along the river (known locally as "the slough") is peaceful, dipping through wetlands and under the shade of cottonwood and alder trees.

At 0.5 mile, turn right to cross the bridge back across the river, following signs for Sammamish River Trail. Ahead, you'll see the trestle-turned-trail portion of the Burke-Gilman. From this perspective, it's easy to see that both trails were once the tracks of railroad through the area. Bothell was originally a logging town, and a hub for steamboats and trains on their way to Seattle via Lake Washington's north shore. This section of trail has the steepest grade (though not too steep) as it climbs to meet up with the Burke-Gilman Trail at 0.7 mile.

A cyclist on the Sammamish River Trail.

Turn right onto the Burke-Gilman and enter the Wayne Tunnel. Until 2014, this tunnel was just stark white. That all changed when local artist Kristen Ramirez created the colorful mural, "Ebb & Flow." The bright orange, yellow, purple, and magenta design are sure to inspire a smile and make for a great photo opportunity; just make sure you watch for cyclists!

After exiting the tunnel, you'll come to the parking areas for Red Brick Road Park and Wayne Golf Course. On the left, is the former Wayne Golf Course. Head across the parking lot to meet up with the former golf course path. Fully acquired by the City of Bothell in December 2018, the former public course is now the city's largest park. A park in its infancy, the trails through this area are not officially defined yet, though community members have retraced the former course paths to create a meandering 0.8-mile loop.

Opened in 1931, the Wayne Golf Course was many community members' first introduction to golf. Loop through the park, to the first of two crossings over the Sammamish River. To the right, you'll spy the moorage at Blue Heron Landing. Once across the bridge, turn left and continue following the curve of the river bank. Other former cart tracks wander up the hillside beyond, abutting a mature forest of Douglas fir and big leaf maple. You'll come again to a bridge at 1.6 miles; turn left to cross the bridge, continuing straight to meet up with the parking lot and closing the Wayne Golf Course loop. Follow the Burke-Gilman back through the Wayne Tunnel to return to Bothell Landing.

Going Further: From Wayne Golf Course, continue on the Burke-Gilman Trail for 2.0 miles into Kenmore. Here, you can brewery-hop between each of the three craft breweries on Kenmore Brewery Row.

The Sammamish River Trail runs over 10 miles from Bothell to Marymoor Park in Redmond as part of the "Locks to Lakes Corridor." Walk, jog, or cycle as far as you like.

Bothell's first schoolhouse on site at Bothell Landing Park.

MILES AND DIRECTIONS

0.0 Beginning near the restrooms, walk east into Bothell Landing Park. After passing the amphitheater, head south across the bridge.

0.1 Turn right onto the Sammamish River Trail.

0.5 Turn right and cross the bridge. Then turn left to stay on the Sammamish River Trail.

0.7 Come to an intersection with the Burke-Gilman Trail. Turn right and continue through the tunnel.

0.8 At the end of the tunnel, turn left (south) and cross the parking lot into the former Wayne Golf Course. Follow the gravel path into the park.

0.9 At the end of the gravel path, continue walking through the grass on an old golf cart track between the river and the treeline.

1.2 Turn left and cross the bridge. At the end of the bridge, turn left to follow the river south.

1.6 Cross the bridge and continue following the grassy path northeast.

1.8 Reach the Burke-Gilman Trail. Turn right to return the way you came through the tunnel.

LOCAL INTEREST

The Guest House Restaurant: Enjoy a warm welcome to the neighborhood at this friendly eatery. Try the polenta! Address: 6810 NE 153rd Place, Kenmore, WA; Phone: (425) 402-4990; Web: www.theguesthouserestaurant.com/

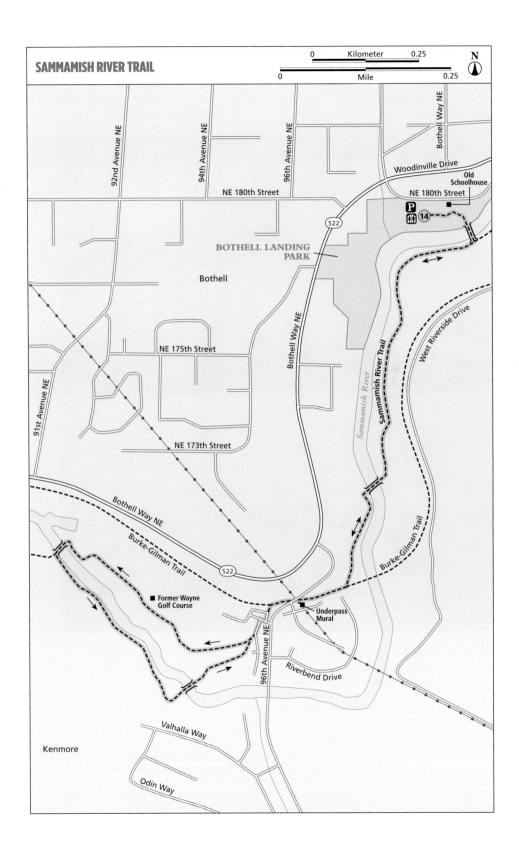

SAMMAMISH RIVER TRAIL

0   Kilometer   0.25

0   Mile   0.25

N

92nd Avenue NE

94th Avenue NE

96th Avenue NE

Bothell Way NE

Woodinville Drive

Old Schoolhouse

NE 180th Street

NE 180th Street

P

14

522

BOTHELL LANDING PARK

Bothell

Bothell Way NE

West Riverside Drive

NE 175th Street

91st Avenue NE

Sammamish River

Sammamish River Trail

NE 173rd Street

Bothell Way NE

Burke-Gilman Trail

Burke-Gilman Trail

522

Former Wayne Golf Course

Underpass Mural

96th Avenue NE

Riverbend Drive

Valhalla Way

Kenmore

Odin Way

A bridge over the Sammamish River at the former Wayne Golf Course.

Cairn Brewing: A family and dog friendly craft brewery located just steps away from the Burke-Gilman Trail. Address: 7204 NE 175th St., Kenmore, WA; Phone: (425) 949-5295; Web: www.cairnbrewing.com

LODGING

McMenamins Anderson School: Located in a historic former high school, the hotel grounds include multiple bars, a brewery, saltwater pool, and movie theater. Address: 18607 Bothell Way NE, Bothell, WA; Phone: (425) 398-0122; Web: www.mcmenamins .com/anderson-school

15 WASHINGTON PARK ARBORETUM

Stroll down scenic Azalea Way and experience Washington Arboretum in bloom: from cherry blossoms in the spring to winter-blooming camellias, there's always something growing.

Elevation gain: 130 feet
Distance: 2.2-mile loop
Hiking time: 1-2 hours
Difficulty: Easy
Seasons: Year round
Trail surface: Packed gravel, paved path
Land status: City park
Nearest town: Seattle
Other users: Joggers, cyclists
Water availability: Yes, at restrooms

Canine compatibility: Dogs must remain on leash
Fees and permits: None
Map: University of Washington Botanic Gardens
Trail contact: University of Washington Botanic Gardens: (206) 543-8800
Trailhead GPS: N47°38.389' W122°17.656'

FINDING THE TRAILHEAD

From I-5, take exit 168B for WA-520 toward Bellevue/Kirkland. Drive 0.5 mile, then take the Montlake Blvd exit. Continue straight onto E Lake Washington Boulevard. Drive 0.5 mile, then turn left onto E Foster Island Road. After 0.1 mile turn right onto Arboretum Drive E and continue to the parking area.

WHAT TO SEE

Wedged between the bustle of downtown Seattle and the shores of Lake Washington, Washington Park Arboretum welcomes visitors with botanic highlights all year round. Jointly operated by Seattle Parks and Recreation and the University of Washington, the park's 230 acres feature native woody plants as well as the newer Pacific Connections Garden. This suggested loop includes the famed Azalea Way, and hits many of the park's collections so that there is always something in bloom no matter what time of year you visit.

Start at the Graham Visitors Center to grab a map and fill up your water bottle. Directly behind the visitor center, cross an access road to start out on the wide pathway of Azalea Way. Combined with the Lookout Gazebo, Azalea Way was the highlight of the original Olmsted Brothers design. Featuring flowering cherries, dogwoods, magnolias and an understory of thousands of azaleas, the 0.75-mile-long trail is at its best in spring. In early April you're likely to see couples and families picnicking under the cherry trees. By Mother's Day weekend in May, the azaleas are in full bloom and turn the stroll technicolor with their varied blooms.

After strolling Azalea Way, you'll briefly turn onto the paved Loop Trail and head up the hill. At 2 miles long, this paved trail is a favorite for joggers and cyclists. This section of the Loop Trail curves around the side slope of the still in-progress Pacific Connections Garden. Look for the signed entrance to this garden to the left and turn to head up the gravel trail. Pacific Connections Garden will feature five distinct regions—Chile, China,

Cherry blossoms bloom along Azalea Way in early spring.

Australia, New Zealand, and Cascadia—each of which shares a similar climate to Seattle. At the time of writing, only two of the gardens have been planted: New Zealand and Cascadia. Follow the trail or take the stairs to the top of the hill and check out the shelter at the top. Continue through the New Zealand forest, a highlight in the summer, before coming to the Lookout Gazebo.

Overlooking Azalea Way below, the Gazebo is a prime example of 1930s parkitecture style. The stone and wood structure offers a bird's-eye view of the flowering trees and shrubs below, and represents an oft-repeated Olmsted motif. The firm designed many of their parks to include a high point such as this that gave visitors a glimpse of the sur- rounding landscape outside the park. From the gazebo head up the stairs to take the upper half of the Lookout Loop through the towering camellia collection. Identified by the pine cone marker on each trail sign, the Lookout Loop traverses the shady and quiet wooded section of the park; a stark contrast to the bustle of Azalea Way downslope. Side paths abound through this section, but all tend to meander in the same general direc- tion, meeting back up with main paths eventually. The Lookout Trail also traverses the arboretum's Asiatic Maples collection, a fall favorite set ablaze in red and orange come late September.

At the far end of the loop, continue straight across a wooden bridge toward the Woodland Gardens and Winter Gardens. A pocket of life while much of the rest of the arboretum sleeps through the chillier months, this garden features Chinese witch hazel, hellebores, and sweetly scented daphne. Explore the garden, encircled by towering cedar trees, or have a seat for a rest on one of the many benches. Then continue on the main path back to the visitor center.

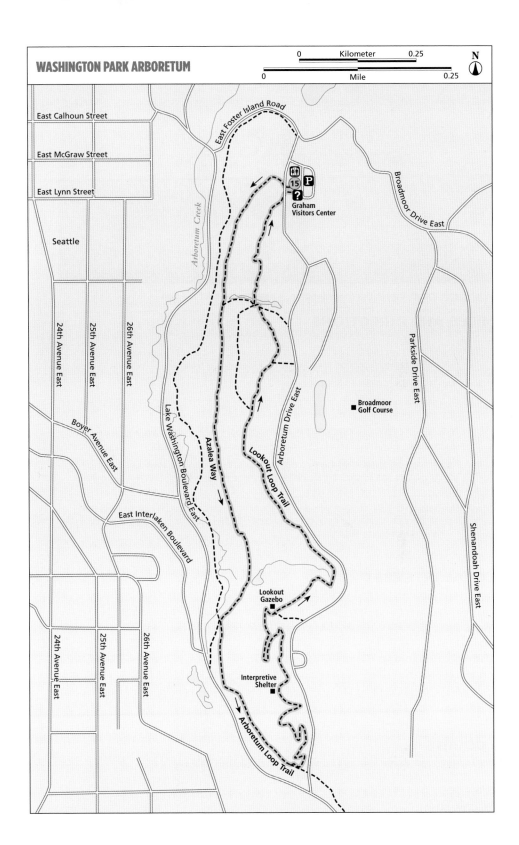

Kilometer
0
0.25

Mile
0
0.25

N

East Calhoun Street

East McGraw Street

East Lynn Street

Seattle

East Foster Island Road

Arboretum Creek

24th Avenue East

25th Avenue East

26th Avenue East

Boyer Avenue East

Lake Washington Boulevard East

Azalea Way

Lookout Loop Trail

Arboretum Drive East

Broadmoor Drive East

Parkside Drive East

Shenandoah Drive East

Graham
Visitors Center

15
P

Broadmoor
Golf Course

East Interlaken Boulevard

24th Avenue East

25th Avenue East

26th Avenue East

Lookout
Gazebo

Interpretive
Shelter

Arboretum Loop Trail

Washington's state flower, the rhodedendron, is seen throughout the park.

MILES AND DIRECTIONS

0.0 Beginning from the Graham Visitors Center, walk west across Arboretum Drive to reach the Azalea Way trail. Head south on the signed trail.

0.7 Turn left onto the paved Loop Trail.

0.9 At a signed junction, turn left for the Pacific Connections Garden. Follow the trail (or take the stairs) through the garden.

1.2 Turn left on Loop Trail to reach the Pacific Connections shelter. After passing the shelter, turn left at the next junction to reach the Lookout Gazebo.

1.4 Reach the Lookout Gazebo. Head up the stairs, then turn left at an unsigned junction to access the Lookout Trail. Follow pine cone markers to stay on the Lookout Trail.

2.0 Head down the stairs, turn left, and walk north across a small bridge toward the Winter Garden. Continue through the Winter Garden, following the path north back to the Graham Visitors Center.

LOCAL INTEREST

Japanese Garden: Located in Washington Park, Seattle Japanese Garden hosts a variety of cultural events open to the public for a nominal admission. Address: 1075 Lake Washington Blvd. East, Seattle, WA; Phone: (206) 684-4725; Web: www.seattlejapanese garden.org

Bamboo Restaurant: Casual Vietnamese fare in the Capitol Hill neighborhood. With vegetarian options available, we recommend the vermicelli bowls. Address: 345 15th Ave. E, Seattle, WA; Phone: (206) 567-3399, Web: www.facebook.com/pg/bamboorestaurant on15

LODGING

For lodging options in Seattle, visit www.visitseattle.org/lodging.

16 ALKI TRAIL

A beachside stroll and epic views of the Seattle skyline make Alki Beach a favorite for locals and visitors alike.

Elevation gain: Minimal
Distance: 4.7 miles out-and-back
Hiking time: 2 hours
Difficulty: Easy
Seasons: Year round
Trail surface: Paved path
Land status: City park
Nearest town: West Seattle Junction
Other users: Cyclists, joggers
Water availability: Yes, at restrooms

Canine compatibility: Dogs must remain on leash, and must stay on trail. Dogs are not allowed at Seattle beaches.
Fees and permits: None
Map: Seattle Parks and Recreation
Trail contact: Seattle Parks and Recreation: (206) 684-4075
Trailhead GPS: N47°34.760′ W122°24.636′

FINDING THE TRAILHEAD

From I-5, take exit 163 for West Seattle Bridge. Drive 2 miles across the bridge, then exit onto SW Admiral Way. Continue on SW Admiral Way for 2.4 miles, then turn right onto 61st Avenue SW. Continue 0.2 mile to reach the intersection with Alki Avenue SW. Street parking is available on 61st Avenue SW and Alki Avenue SW. Once parked, walk down the steps north of Alki Avenue SW to begin your hike from Statue of Liberty Plaza.

WHAT TO SEE

Alki, the unofficial motto of Washington State, comes from Chinook jargon and roughly translates to "by and by," or eventually. But if you asked most Washingtonians about Alki, they would undoubtedly think only of the stretch of beach in West Seattle on Alki Point. On sunny summer weekends, the beach overflows with Seattleite sun worshipers, getting in a game of beach volleyball or exploring tidepools at low tide. It's also one of two beaches where bonfires are allowed within the city of Seattle (just make sure to keep them in the designated fire pits). The full Alki Trail runs from the base of the West Seattle Bridge to the far west end of Alki Beach. The route described here takes you from the iconic Statue of Liberty Plaza to Seacrest Park and back, covering points of interest while leaving plenty of time to hit the beach!

From Statue of Liberty Plaza, located centrally along the beach promenade, head out on the wide paved pathway northeast. This miniature replica of the iconic New York landmark was donated by the Boy Scouts in 1952 and has become a beloved local landmark in its own right. You'll soon come to the Alki Beach Bathhouse, where restrooms are available. The Bathhouse itself is now home to an artist studio and event space.

The Alki Trail is a popular promenade, and on summer days turns into Seattle's answer to Santa Monica Pier. You might share the wide path with rollerbladers, families on bikes, or joggers. Across the street you'll see colorful bungalows, and many of West Seattle's favorite restaurants. After passing the volleyball courts, the beach becomes rockier, and views across Elliott Bay are often decorated by passing ferries. Orcas and humpbacks are sometimes seen in the bay off Alki, earning the beach a designation on the Whale Trail. Harbor seals will often sun themselves on the beach. If you spot a seal pup that seems to

The Seattle skyline as seen from Alki Trail.

be alone, don't worry. Mothers will often leave their pups on a safe, warm beach in order to go fishing on their own. Give the animals plenty of room and don't disturb them.

If visiting during low tide, you might spot all that remains of Luna Park (now known as Anchor Park) just off the Duwamish Head. Once an amusement park modeled after Coney Island, in 1931 the structure succumbed to a fire that destroyed everything, leaving only the remnants of pilings. This is just one of the many fascinating and colorful stories of Alki's past. Not the least of those tales is the point's importance as the landing site for Seattle's first white settlers. The Denny Party travelled nine months along the Oregon Trail from Illinois to Portland, OR, before sailing north to Alki aboard the schooner *Exact*. They arrived "rain-soaked and seasick" before eventually moving on to settle at Pioneer Square—the oldest of Seattle's neighborhoods.

As you round Duwamish Head, the downtown skyline will come into view. This is the perspective of the city most tourists are familiar with—The Space Needle and Columbia Tower appear to rise straight out of Puget Sound, and on clear days you'll spot Mount Rainier looming in the distance. For city views that just keep getting better, stick to the trail along the water's edge as it crosses through the boat launch. A few pocket parks and viewpoints allow for plenty of photo opportunities.

The turnaround point for this trail is Seacrest Park. Grab a bite to eat from local favorite Marination Station, or hop a water taxi into downtown from the dock at the park. Or simply head back the way you came to enjoy more time on the beach. Alki is for strolling and relaxing, knowing you'll get to your destination "by and by."

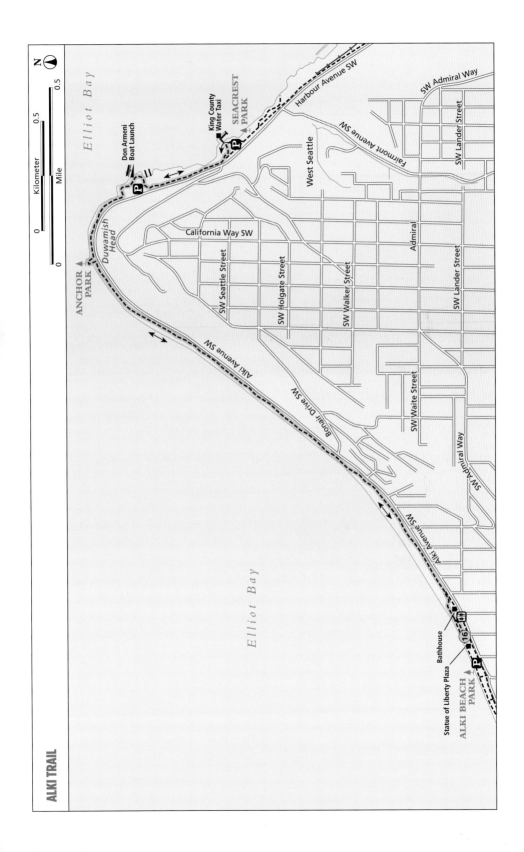

ALKI TRAIL

N

Kilometer
0   0.5

Mile
0   0.5

Elliot Bay

Elliot Bay

ANCHOR PARK

Duwamish Head

Don Armeni Boat Launch

King County Water Taxi

SEACREST PARK

Harbour Avenue SW

Fairmont Avenue SW

West Seattle

California Way SW

SW Seattle Street

SW Holgate Street

SW Walker Street

Admiral

SW Lander Street

SW Admiral Way

SW Lander Street

Bonair Drive SW

Alki Avenue SW

Alki Avenue SW

SW Waite Street

SW Admiral Way

Statue of Liberty Plaza

Bathhouse

ALKI BEACH PARK

16

Harbor seals are often seen off the coast of Alki and mothers will leave pups to warm on the shore.

MILES AND DIRECTIONS

0.0 From the Statue of Liberty Plaza at Alki Beach Park, walk northeast on the Alki Trail along the shoreline.

1.6 Reach Anchor Park at Duwamish Head, and walk out on the dock for Seattle skyline views. Then continue east on the Alki Trail.

1.9 Turn left (east) at a junction to follow the trail along the shoreline. Then continue south along the Alki Trail.

2.3 Reach Seacrest Park and pier. Enjoy the views, then return the way you came.

LOCAL INTEREST

Alki Point Lighthouse: This active Coast Guard lighthouse, constructed in 1913, offers free Sunday afternoon tours during summer. Located 0.2 miles from the west end of the Alki Trail, some road-walking (or a short drive) required. Address: 3201 Alki Ave. SW, Seattle, WA; Email: alkilighthouse@cgauxseattle.org; Web: www.cgauxseattle.org

Lincoln Park: Another classic West Seattle park, Lincoln Park offers over 4 miles of forested walking trails, beaches, bluffs, and a heated saltwater pool. Address: 8011 Fauntleroy Way SW, Seattle, WA; Phone: (206) 684-4075; Web: www.seattle.gov/parks/find/parks/lincoln-park

LODGING

For lodging options in Seattle, visit www.visitseattle.org/lodging.

17 DISCOVERY PARK LOOP

Seattle's Discovery Park is an urban hiker's dream: both wild and accessible, its 534 acres include forest, meadow, beach, and bluff all connected by miles of trails. Come for the fresh air and stay for expansive Olympic Mountain views across Puget Sound.

Elevation gain: 490 feet
Distance: 4.4-mile loop
Hiking time: 2 hours
Difficulty: Moderate
Seasons: Year round
Trail surface: Paved path, gravel, dirt path
Land status: City park
Nearest town: Seattle
Other users: Joggers, cyclists
Water availability: Yes, at restrooms

Canine compatibility: Dogs must remain on leash, and must stay on-trail. Dogs are not allowed at Seattle beaches.
Fees and permits: None
Map: Friends of Discovery Park
Trail contact: Seattle Parks and Recreation: (206) 684-4075
Trailhead GPS: N47°39.281' W122°24.625'

FINDING THE TRAILHEAD

From Exit 169 on I-5, head west on NE 50th St for 1.5 miles. Turn left onto Phinney Avenue N, then immediately turn right onto N 49th Street. Drive 0.2 mile, then turn right onto NW Market Street. Drive 1 mile, then turn left onto 15th Avenue NW. Drive 1 mile, crossing over the Ballard Bridge, then turn right onto W Emerson Street. Drive 0.5 mile, then turn right onto Gilman Avenue W. Drive 0.5 mile, then continue onto W Government Way. Drive 0.4 mile, then turn left onto 34th Avenue W. Drive 0.4 mile, then turn right onto W Emerson Street. Finally, drive 0.6 mile, then turn right onto Carolina Street to reach the South Parking Lot.

WHAT TO SEE

You could spend days exploring Seattle's largest city park. Many locals do just that—residents of the Magnolia neighborhood lucky enough to call Discovery Park their backyard can be found strolling its extensive trail network nearly every week. Visitors flock here as well for iconic mountain-and-sound views from the West Point Lighthouse. Located just 5 miles from Seattle Center, Discovery Park provides a sanctuary for wildlife and nature-seekers near the heart of the city.

Set out on the popular 2.8-mile Loop Trail to experience the best of Discovery Park. Think of the loop as a wheel, with spokes (various trails) leading out to the park's attractions. From the South Parking Lot, walk west (clockwise) around the loop. The first 0.3 miles parallel Emerson Street along a wooded path, but you'll soon leave the sound of traffic behind as the trail opens up to a grassy lawn. Visible to the north is the Fort Lawton Historic Area—a reminder that Discovery Park's grounds were formerly used as a military base. Continue following Loop Trail to reach unobstructed bluff-top views of the Olympic Mountains at 0.5 miles.

The first 0.8 miles of the Loop Trail are easygoing, with ever-improving views of Puget Sound from Magnolia Bluff. But to fully experience Discovery Park, you have to hike to the beach. Hang a left on the South Beach Trail to drop over 200 feet down a series of stairs. You'll pass by a couple of (somewhat overgrown) overlook platforms

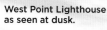

along the way. Unlike the Loop Trail, the South Beach Trail is steep, narrow, and at times rooty—a true hiking trail with peek-a-boo views to Bainbridge Island across the Sound. Surrounded by forest, fringe cups, and nettles, this section of trail feels truly wild.

Once you reach the beach, head out to West Point Lighthouse—the westernmost point in all of Seattle. Originally constructed in 1881, the lighthouse is still active today—a navigational landmark for ferries and ships passing through Puget Sound. Visit during sunset for the most dramatic photo opportunities. When the weather is clear here, Mount Rainier rises above Seattle's southern skyline, bathed in alpenglow at nightfall. This scene is as Seattle as it gets. With saltwater at your feet, historic lighthouse by your side and volcano views beyond, Discovery Park proves itself a world-class urban hiking destination.

Climb from sea level back up the bluffs to the Loop Trail to finish your circuit. The trail zigzags through the park, rolling with gentle elevation gain and loss as it circles back to the South Parking Lot. Catch a glimpse of the Fort Lawton Military Cemetery at 3.8 miles before taking the pedestrian tunnel beneath Discovery Park Boulevard. Shortly thereafter you'll reach a junction with the East Parking Lot and Environmental Learning Center—a good place to stop for a bathroom break and information on educational park programs. From here you're on the home stretch—a pleasant walk through the Emerald City's evergreen forest back to your car.

MILES AND DIRECTIONS

- **0.0** From the south end of the South Parking Lot, walk west on the signed, gravel Loop Trail.
- **0.4** A short side path leads to restrooms and water. Continue on the Loop Trail.
- **0.6** Reach the Sandy Area. Stay left on the Loop Trail.

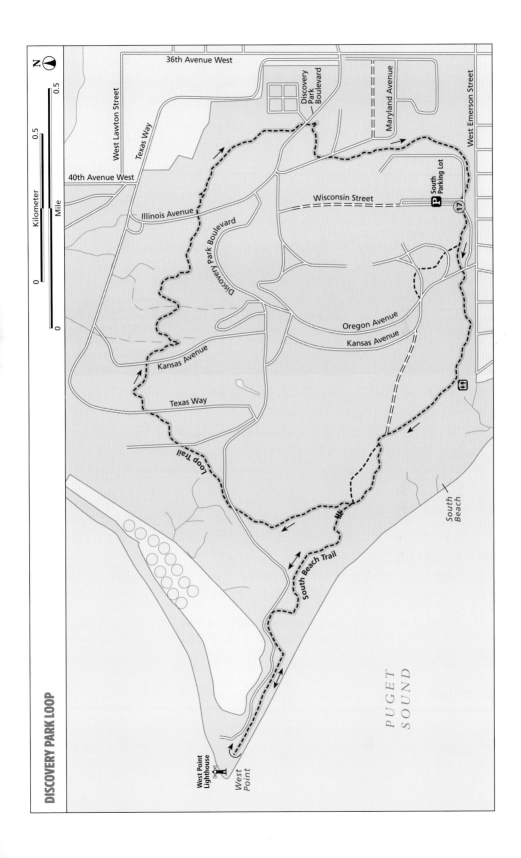

DISCOVERY PARK LOOP

A bench on the bluffs overlooking Puget Sound on the Loop Trail.

0.8 Turn left onto the South Beach Trail and take the steps down.

1.1 Turn right at a junction with bluff views.

1.2 Turn left at Discovery Park Boulevard and walk the sidewalk down to the beach.

1.3 Turn right to walk out along the shoreline.

1.5 Reach the West Point Lighthouse. Turn around here and retrace your steps to the Loop Trail.

2.3 Turn left onto the Loop Trail. Continue following signs for the Loop Trail back to the South Parking Lot.

LOCAL INTEREST

Ballard Locks: Visit the busiest locks in the nation to watch watercraft of all sizes traveling between the saltwater of Puget Sound and freshwater of Lake Union and Lake Washington. Cross the ship canal by swinging walkway from Magnolia to reach the Carl S. English Jr. Botanical Garden and access Old Ballard. Park for free at Commodore Park. Address: 3015 NW 54th Street, Seattle, WA; Phone: (206) 783-7059; Web: www .ballardlocks.org

LODGING

For lodging options in Seattle, visit www.visitseattle.org/lodging.

18 WILBURTON HILL PARK

Home to serene nature trails, a 150-foot-long suspension bridge, and the Bellevue Botanical Garden, Wilburton Hill Park is an urban refuge at the edge of downtown Bellevue.

Elevation gain: 200 feet
Distance: 2-mile double loop
Hiking time: 1-2 hours
Difficulty: Easy
Seasons: Year round
Trail surface: Gravel path, paved path, dirt trail
Land status: City park
Nearest town: Bellevue
Other users: Joggers
Water availability: Yes, at restrooms
Canine compatibility: Dogs are not permitted in the botanical garden.

Dogs must remain on leash in the rest of the park.
Fees and permits: None
Map: Wilburton Hill Park Trail - City of Bellevue: www.bellevuewa.gov/city-government/departments/parks/parks-and-trails/nature-trails/wilburton-hill-park-trail
Trail contact: City of Bellevue Parks: (425) 452-6885
Trailhead GPS: N47.6095 W122.1743

FINDING THE TRAILHEAD

From I-405, take exit 13B for NE 8th Street East. Drive east for 0.6 mile on NE 8th Street. Turn right onto 124th Avenue NE, then drive 0.5 mile. Turn left into the signed parking lot at Wilburton Hill Park. Begin your hike from the northeast corner of the lot, near the restrooms.

WHAT TO SEE

Whether you're seeking respite from I-405 traffic or simply looking for "things to do" in Bellevue, the Bellevue Botanical Garden should be at the top of your to-do list. Free to enter, these beautifully landscaped gardens are a favorite spot to wander for locals and visitors alike. Turn your garden stroll into an urban hike by beginning across the park and making your way into the gardens.

Looking at a map of Wilburton Hill (pick one up at the botanical garden visitor center), you'll notice that the park is divided into two rectangular sections. The east part of the park is home to a picnic area, playground, baseball fields, and nature trails. The Bellevue Botanical Garden makes up the west side of the park, with 53 acres of Pacific Northwest plants, woodlands, and wetlands. We suggest hiking Wilburton Hill Park from east to west for the full experience—from quiet wooded trails to gardens bursting with seasonal colors.

Begin your hike by walking around Wilburton Hill Park's northernmost baseball field. Watch out for pop flies and home runs! The dirt path climbs gently as it encircles the outfield, then drops into the forest. Madrone trees guard the entrance to a lush nature trail full of towering big leaf maples. Pretty soon you'll meet the wide, gravel Lake to Lake Trail. This 10-mile long greenway connects Lake Sammamish to Lake Washington via a series of parks, with Wilburton right in the middle. Opportunities to explore along this long urban trail are seemingly endless. For now, make your way past the playground and soccer field to explore the heart of Wilburton Hill Park: Bellevue Botanical Garden.

A kiosk welcomes users to the gardens, explaining a few rules and providing a helpful map. Note that pets and wheels (bikes, skateboards, etc.) are not allowed inside. Enter through the Yao Garden's traditional Japanese gate and you'll suddenly be surrounded by azaleas, rhododendrons, and Japanese maples—plants and trees found in both Bellevue and its sister city of Yao, Japan. From here, take the wide and easygoing Tateuchi Loop Trail for access to the core gardens. Along this trail, you may notice signposts reading "tap or scan." Smartphone users can connect to the city of Bellevue's free WiFi network, then use NFC technology or a QR code to access the park's electronic plant database.

Highlights of the Tateuchi Loop Trail are abundant, from small waterfalls trickling into koi ponds to the Tateuchi Pavilion, the Shorts House, and more cultivated gardens. Stop by the Shorts House—built in 1957—for access to a reference library, cafe, and visitor information from the atrium. You can also drop down to the botanical gardens' main entrance from here to shop at the Trillium store (proceeds go back to the park). Continue around the loop to see the Rock Garden (mountain hemlock and wildflowers), Fuschia Garden, and additional themed gardens throughout. Then head south on the Lost Meadow Trail, plunging into comparatively quiet, dense forest for the Ravine Experience.

Second-growth forest provides a dramatic backdrop for the 150-foot suspension bridge spanning this ravine. It's a unique site in an otherwise urban area, surrounded by homes, industry, and roads on every side. But the forest provides a remarkably effective buffer from the city, and you'll momentarily forget how close you are to downtown Bellevue as you cross this picturesque bridge. From here it's just 0.5 miles back to the trailhead at Wilburton Hill Park.

Going Further: From Wilburton Park, follow the Lake to Lake Trail west along Main Street to Bellevue's Downtown Park. Walk around the park's canal for nice views of its 240-foot-wide waterfall and pond. Alternatively, you can head south on the Lake to Lake Trail to Mercer Slough Nature Park (see Hike #19). Or walk east on the greenway to Kelsey Creek Nature Park and Lake Sammamish beyond.

MILES AND DIRECTIONS

0.0   From the trailhead near the restrooms, walk east on the wide paved path. Just past the restrooms, turn left onto a signed dirt trail.

0.2   Enter the forest north of the baseball fields. Stay right at the next three trail junctions.

0.4   Turn left (south) at a junction. Then turn right (west) onto the wide gravel Lake to Lake Trail.

0.6   Continue past the playground on the Lake to Lake Trail. Turn left (south) at the soccer field.

0.8   Reach the Bellevue Botanical Garden's Yao Garden entrance. Enter the gardens here.

0.9   Meet the wide Tateuchi Loop Trail. Walk northwest on this trail for a clockwise loop.

1.0   Reach the Shorts House. Continue north along Tateuchi Loop Trail.

1.2   Turn right on the Lost Meadow Trail for the Ravine Experience.

1.5   Turn right and cross the suspension bridge.

1.7   Turn left (north) to return to the playground. Then walk north to reach the trailhead at 2 miles.

A suspension bridge traverses a ravine in the wooded section of the park.

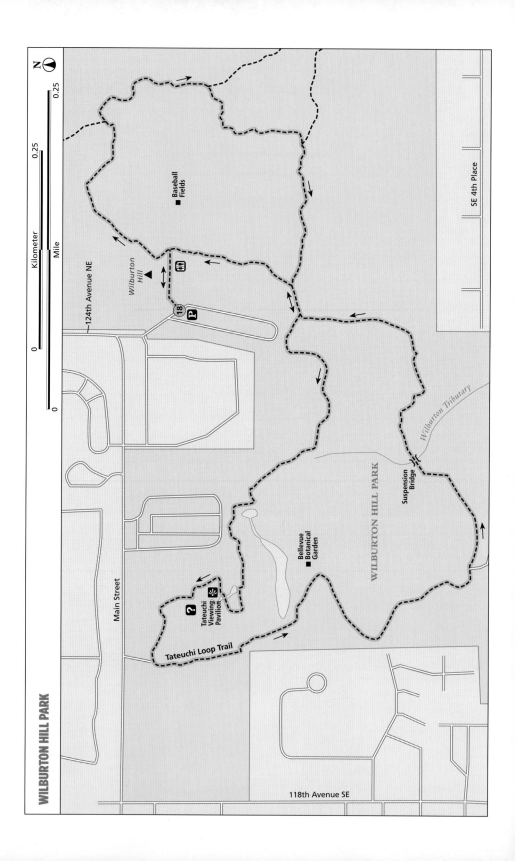

WILBURTON HILL PARK

N

Kilometer
0   0.25   0.25

Mile
0   0.25

124th Avenue NE

Main Street

118th Avenue SE

SE 4th Place

Wilburton Hill

■ Baseball
  Fields

Tateuchi Loop Trail

Tateuchi Viewing Pavilion

■ Bellevue
  Botanical
  Garden

WILBURTON HILL PARK

Suspension Bridge

Wilburton Tributary

The trails on Wilburton Hill traverse mature forests.

LOCAL INTEREST

Copper Kettle Coffee Bar: Located inside the Shorts House at Bellevue Botanical Garden, this humble cafe offers pastries and coffee with unbeatable garden views from the patio. Address: 12001 Main St., Bellevue, WA; Phone: (425) 452-2750; Web: www .bellevuebotanical.org/garden-cafe

LODGING

Hotel 116: At just 1 mile from Wilburton Hill Park, this three-star hotel is the obvious choice for out-of-towners. Address: 625 116th Avenue NE, Bellevue, WA; Phone: (425) 455-9444; Web: www.coasthotels.com/hotels/washington/hotel-116-a-coast-hotel-bellevue

19 MERCER SLOUGH HERITAGE LOOP

Explore the largest remaining wetland on Lake Washington for a chance at wildlife sightings, and the unique opportunity to explore a working historic blueberry farm.

Elevation gain: 150 feet
Distance: 2.6-mile double loop
Hiking time: 1–2 hours
Difficulty: Easy-moderate due to stairs and short, steep trail sections
Seasons: Year round
Trail surface: Gravel path, dirt trail, boardwalk
Land status: City park
Nearest town: Bellevue
Other users: Joggers, cyclists
Water availability: Yes, at restrooms

Canine compatibility: Dogs must remain on leash
Fees and permits: None
Map: Mercer Slough Nature Park Trail Map - City of Bellevue: www .bellevuewa.gov/city-government/ departments/parks/parks-and-trails/ nature-trails/mercer-slough-nature-park-trails
Trail contact: City of Bellevue Parks: (425) 452-6885
Trailhead GPS: N47.5965 W122.1832

FINDING THE TRAILHEAD

From I-405, take exit 12 for SE 8th Street. Turn west onto SE 8th Street, then immediately turn south (left) onto 118th Avenue SE. Drive 0.4 mile, then turn right into the signed park entrance for Mercer Slough Environmental Education Center.

WHAT TO SEE

The largest remaining wetland on Lake Washington, Mercer Slough Nature Park has 320 acres that can be explored on foot or by paddle. Within a few short steps from the trailhead, you'll easily forget that this wildlife oasis is in the middle of the bustling city of Bellevue. Bisected by Mercer Slough, the park has two distinct sections: the wild scrub-shrub wetlands to the east, and the historic blueberry farms to the west. Take in both sides of the park along this 2.6-mile double loop hike.

Start your hike by exploring the Environmental Education Center campus. Jointly run by Pacific Science Center and Bellevue Parks, the complex houses classrooms and a visitor center. Stop in to chat with a ranger if visiting during the summer months. The buildings are sustainably built, their living roofs blending in with forest around them. After passing the treehouse, head down the steps to embark on the Bellefields Loop Trail. This first section of trail through the forested area of the park is a bit of a roller coaster. Some sections of steep trails will get your blood pumping and may prove challenging for young hikers. Soon, however, the dirt trail transitions to boardwalk as you enter the wetlands.

The stark change between the forest and wetlands is almost immediate as the towering Douglas firs are replaced by shrubs, cattails, and cottonwoods. Keep your eyes peeled for frogs in the marsh along the trail, or maybe even a beaver. Since over 170 different species of plants and animals call this area home, each visit to the park will seem like a new

The Bellefields Loop is connected to the Heritage Loop via a bridge over Mercer Slough.

A cottontail rabbit scurries into the brush near the elevated boardwalk.

experience. During our visit we sighted a handful of frogs, and even a cottontail rabbit along this section of trail.

At just over 0.6 miles, you'll cross Mercer Slough. An easily accessible spot to kayak or canoe, this peaceful waterway is a popular recreation area. Boat rentals are available at nearby Enatai Beach Park and the Bellevue Parks offer guided tours on Saturday mornings May through October. After crossing the bridge, you'll come to the Heritage Trail. This trail wanders around the historic Mercer Slough Blueberry Farm. This farm, along with the Larsen Lake Blueberry Farm, are managed by the city and offer U-pick opportunities in the summer—check ahead of your visit to learn more. The rows of sprawling bushes are a lush green in the summer, turning crimson as the crisp kiss of autumn takes hold. Even the skeletal branches of the bushes in the winter make for a picturesque landscape.

After circling the farm, return to the bridge and cross back over the slough to complete the second half of the Bellefields Loop. Paralleling the slough, this part of the trail offers some of the best odds for wildlife sightings. The transition from shrub-scrub to forest is seemingly more gradual on this second half of the loop, and in a blink it seems you'll be back at the base of the Environmental Learning Center.

Going Further: As a part of the Lake to Lake trail system, it's possible to hike to Wilburton Hill and the Bellevue Botanical Gardens from here. Alternately, seasonal kayak and canoe rentals are available through REI at Enatai Beach on Lake Washington, which would allow for a third trail through the park: The Canoe Trail.

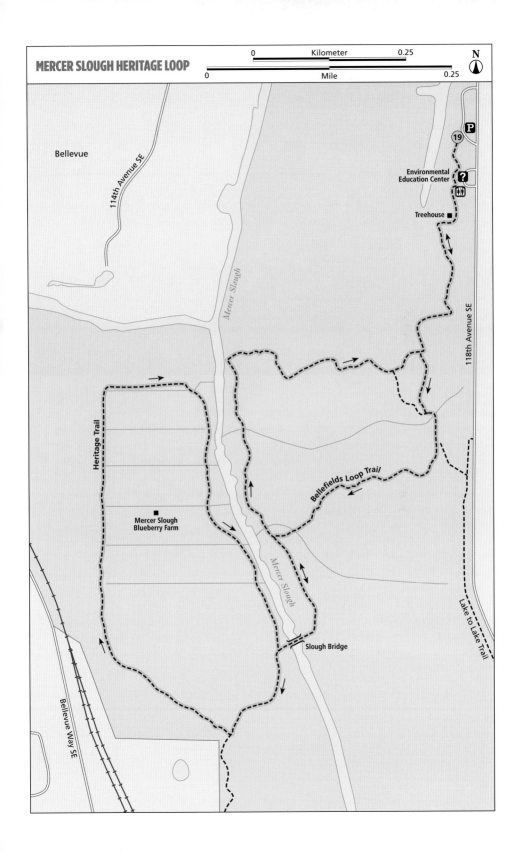

MERCER SLOUGH HERITAGE LOOP

Kilometer
0   0.25

Mile
0   0.25

N

Bellevue

114th Avenue SE

Mercer Slough

P

19

Environmental
Education Center

?

Treehouse ■

118th Avenue SE

Heritage Trail

Bellefields Loop Trail

■ Mercer Slough
Blueberry Farm

Mercer Slough

Slough Bridge

Lake to Lake Trail

Bellevue Way SE

Trees in the wetland create a tunnel-like experience on the trail.

MILES AND DIRECTIONS

0.0 Beginning from the kiosk in the upper parking lot, walk south on the gravel path. Turn left to ascend the stairs to the Environmental Education Center (EEC). Continue walking south along the raised boardwalk.

0.1 Reach the treehouse. Descend the nearby stairs to the trail and turn left to walk south on the dirt path.

0.3 Turn left to go clockwise on the Bellefields Loop Trail. Turn left again at the next junction.

0.4 Turn right at a junction.

0.6 Turn left to exit the Bellefields Loop Trail.

0.8 After crossing the bridge, stay left to hike the Heritage Loop clockwise.

0.9 Turn right, following signs for Overlake Farm.

1.1 Head north, following the trail through the blueberry farm.

1.7 Return across the bridge.

1.9 Turn left to complete the Bellefields Loop Trail.

2.3 Turn left and retrace your steps to the trailhead.

LOCAL INTEREST

City of Bellevue Blueberry Farms: Grab a bucket and get picking! U-pick open when in season. Larsen Lake Blueberry Farms is open for U-pick during Sound Transit Construction near Mercer Slough. Address: 700 148th Ave. SE, Bellevue, WA; Phone: (346) 298-0193; Web: www.bellevuewa.gov/city-government/departments/parks/

REI Boathouse at Enatai Beach Park: Offers SUP, canoe, and kayak rentals on the shores of Lake Washington near the mouth of Mercer Slough. Address: 3519 108th Ave. SE, Bellevue, WA; Phone: (425) 902-9508; Web: www.rei.com/h/enatai-beach-boathouse

LODGING

Residence Inn by Marriott: Close to both downtown and Mercer Slough Nature Park. Address: 605 114th Ave. SE, Bellevue, WA; Phone: (425) 637-8500; Web: www.marriott.com

20 SNOQUALMIE FALLS TRAIL

Take in the view from above and below the stunning 270-foot cascade of Snoqualmie Falls on a short but steep hike, then cool down on the banks of the Snoqualmie River.

Elevation gain: 350 feet
Distance: 1.5 miles out-and-back
Hiking time: 1 hour
Difficulty: Moderate
Seasons: Year round
Trail surface: Gravel, boardwalk, paved path
Land status: Private land (Puget Sound Energy)
Nearest town: Snoqualmie
Other users: None
Water availability: Yes, at restrooms

Canine compatibility: Dogs must remain on leash
Fees and permits: Free parking available at upper and lower lots. Main parking lot requires a paid parking permit.
Map: Green Trails Map 205S Rattlesnake Mountain
Trail contact: Puget Sound Energy: (425) 831-4445
Trailhead GPS: N47°32.730' W121°50.426'

FINDING THE TRAILHEAD

From Seattle, head east on I-90 and take exit 22 for Preston. Cross over the freeway and turn right onto SE Highpoint Way/Preston Fall City Road. Continue 4 miles, coming to a traffic circle after crossing the Snoqualmie River. Take the first exit at the traffic circle onto SR-202 East. Drive 2.3 miles, then turn right onto 372nd Avenue SE. Drive 0.3 mile, then turn slightly left for Southeast Fish Hatchery Road. Continue 0.5 mile to reach the lower parking lot and trailhead.

WHAT TO SEE

An iconic Washington natural landmark, Snoqualmie Falls draws visitors from all around the world. For those lucky enough to find this 270-foot waterfall in their backyard, return visits will allow you to watch as the rushing waters change through the seasons. From a massive curtain of water during heavy rains, to segmented chutes during dry summer months, Snoqualmie Falls will enchant visitors with its many appearances.

Most visitors to Snoqualmie Falls only explore the upper viewing platforms, which on a sunny Saturday will be crowded with families and couples taking waterfall selfies. To avoid some of the crowds and parking madness, make the lower falls parking lot your trailhead. The lower parking lot does see its share of summertime weekend traffic as well—this section of river is a popular starting destination for river floaters. Visit on a weekday, in the morning, or later afternoon for a less crowded experience. Pro-tip: The best time to take pictures of the falls is at sunset.

Begin the hike by heading out past the display of old pentstock and turbines towards the formidable pipes and art deco structure of Power Plant 2. From here, follow the stairs down the boardwalk, which leads out to the lower platform view of the falls. On days when the falls are truly raging, you'll be able to feel the spray from even here. It might be tempting to get a closer view, but stay on the path. The currents of the Snoqualmie River change rapidly and can be deadly. Head back along the boardwalk, and start walking up

Visitors marvel at Snoqualmie Falls from the upper observation deck.

the trail. While a short hike, many unprepared tourists have underestimated its difficulty. Signs at each end of the trail inform visitors that the hill climb is the equivalent of climbing to the top of a 30-story building. Be prepared to share the trail with families, many of whom may be huffing and puffing their way up the hill.

The first section of trail is unshaded and can be quite warm on summer days—make sure you have a full water bottle. As the trail switchbacks up the hill, you'll come into sections of both second-growth and old-growth forests. Take the time to read the interpretive signs along the way while catching your breath. Cedar, Douglas fir, and western hemlock make for a thick canopy above, while the understory is dotted with nurse logs, salmonberry, snowberry, and many others. Look for name plates for the flora, and listen for birdsongs ringing from the branches above.

When you make it to the top, head over to the multiple overlook decks for aerial views of Snoqualmie Falls. Even on weekdays this area is incredibly busy. Snap a few photos, maybe browse the gift shop, and above all take in the majesty of the falls. Head back down the trail when you're satisfied.

Upon reaching the bottom of the hill, head down a pathway just beyond the parking lot signed as "River Access." Here you can clamber down to the rocky, sand shores of the Snoqualmie River. This section of the river is far enough downstream that quick and dramatic water level changes are not as noticeable; however, do be careful as the currents here are swift. Cool off your tired feet in the shallows, explore along the riverbank, or find a sunny rock to eat lunch on. Pack up and head back to your car once you've enjoyed the views.

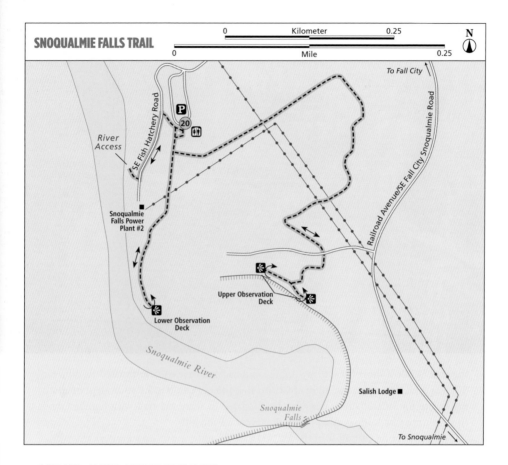

SNOQUALMIE FALLS TRAIL

MILES AND DIRECTIONS

0.0 Begin by walking south from the trailhead towards the lower observation deck.

0.2 Reach the lower observation deck. Turn around and return the way you came.

0.3 Turn right at a junction near the trailhead picnic area to begin hiking uphill.

0.8 Stay to the right on the paved path to reach the upper observation deck. From here, you can walk south a short distance towards the falls to another observation platform.

0.9 Turn around and retrace your steps to the lower parking lot picnic area.

1.3 Turn right, then go left down the stairs. Take a second left when you reach the road to walk down to the river.

1.4 Reach the river access area. Turn around here and retrace your steps to the trailhead.

LOCAL INTEREST

Snoqualmie Falls Hydroelectric Museum: A seasonal fee-free museum chronicling the history of the hydroelectric plant. Address: SE 69th Place, Snoqualmie, WA; Phone: (425) 831-4445; Web: www.pse.com/pages/tours-and-recreation/snoqualmie-tours

Snoqualmie Falls as seen from the lower observation deck.

LODGING

Salish Lodge and Spa: Perched above the falls, this luxury hotel offers a full spa and award-winning restaurant. Address: 6501 Railroad Ave., Snoqualmie, WA; Phone: (425) 888-2556; Web: www.salishlodge.com

21 GENE COULON PARK

Explore the southern tip of Lake Washington at Gene Coulon Memorial Park to experience wetland boardwalks, swimming beaches, and extensive picnic options.

Elevation gain: Minimal
Distance: 2.7 miles out-and-back
Hiking time: 1.5 hours
Difficulty: Easy
Seasons: Year round
Trail surface: Paved path, boardwalk
Land status: City park
Nearest town: Renton
Other users: Joggers

Water availability: At restrooms
Canine compatibility: Dogs prohibited
Fees and permits: None
Map: City of Renton Parks
Trail contact: City of Renton Parks: (425) 430-6600
Trailhead GPS: N47°30.223' W122°12.208'

FINDING THE TRAILHEAD

From Exit 5 on I-405, follow signs for Park Avenue North. Merge onto Southport Drive North and head west. Drive 0.2 mile, then turn right onto Lake Washington Blvd North. Take the first left onto Coulon Beach Acrd/Coulon Beach Park Drive, then continue through a traffic circle to access the south parking lot. Trailhead is at the west end of the lot, near the playground.

WHAT TO SEE

Gene Coulon Memorial Beach Park has gone through many changes through the decades. The 57 acres at the southern end of Lake Washington was first a coal dump, then a log dump, before the first 23 acres were developed into a park in 1968. Originally named Lake Washington Beach Park, the park would be renamed in 1978 for the "legendary" Renton parks director Gene Coulon. Now, the park welcomes visitors looking to swim, boat, jog, or grab dinner at one of two restaurants on the boardwalk.

Start from the general parking at the south end of the park. Taking the main path head first to Bird Island. Restoration for the island took place in 2017, creating this new boardwalk and restoring the natural landscape. Take the boardwalk out to the island and watch for turtles and birds in the marsh. The calm waters of Lake Washington in this area are important habitat for young salmon and Bird Island promotes this further.

Continue on to the swimming beach boardwalk. During the summer, this area is a mess of splashing and kids paddling. After circling the swimming beach, you'll come to the boat launch area. Be careful while crossing the street here and remember that drivers launching or retrieving boats have the right of way. Once across, you'll arrive at the covered picnic area and waterwalk. Also attached to the picnic area is an observatory tower—climb up for a bird's-eye view of the park and south Seattle. You might even want to grab lunch from the beloved Seattle seafood chain Ivar's. Every year during the winter holidays, Ivar's is the sponsor of Clam Lights in Gene Coulon Park. This holiday light display is an annual tradition for many locals. Continue out on the waterwalk for amazing views of Lake Washington, Mount Rainier, and on clear days the Olympic Mountains. There are also a number of floating picnic piers that offer a unique dining experience.

Path along the shores of Lake Washington in Gene Coulon Park.

After finishing the waterwalk, climb the stairs and meet up with the main path to continue on along the grassy shoreline. Ahead you'll see a hill climbing out of the otherwise flat park. This is The Mount, and its grassy slopes offer a sunny spot to sunbathe or read in the park. Cross the trestle marsh and look up at the trees lining this section of path. These are European larches, and unlike most conifers they lose their needles in the winter. In the spring and summer these trees will be a luscious dark green, before changing to golden hues in the fall. Their alpine counterparts have inspired the term "larch madness" as many hikers flood trails in the Cascade Mountains to see them at peak golden hues.

The final stretch of Gene Coulon Park is incredibly peaceful, away from the bustle of the playgrounds and picnic areas. Birders will enjoy the numerous waterfowl that swim along the marshy shores. Once you reach a chain fence with a gate, you will have reached the end of the park. Turn around here and continue back to the southern parking area. For the most part, you will retrace the same path, but instead of walking along the waterwalk, stay on the main path to experience Washington-based humanist sculptor Phillip Levine's "Interface," a distinctive bronze work that stands out on the grassy lawn. Continue back to the parking area, enjoying the views of Mount Rainier on the way.

MILES AND DIRECTIONS

0.0 Begin from the west end of the south parking lot, near restrooms and the playground. Walk northwest around the playground to Bird Island.

0.1 Cross the bridge onto Bird Island. Complete the short lollipop loop, returning to the bridge.

0.2 Follow the shoreline east from Bird Island to reach the swimming dock and walk out along the dock.

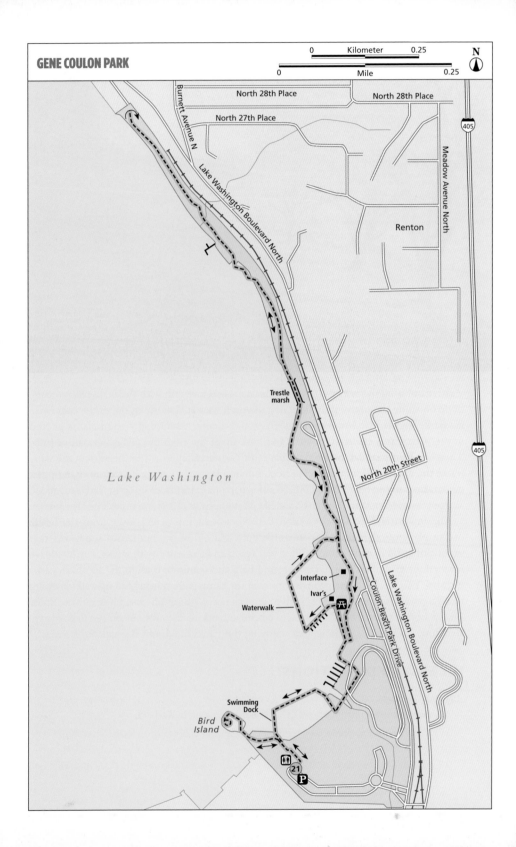

GENE COULON PARK

0 Kilometer 0.25

0 Mile 0.25

N

North 28th Place

North 28th Place

North 27th Place

Burnett Avenue N

Lake Washington Boulevard North

Meadow Avenue North

Renton

Trestle marsh

North 20th Street

Lake Washington

Interface

Ivar's

Waterwalk

Coulon Beach Park Drive

Lake Washington Boulevard North

Swimming Dock

Bird Island

21

P

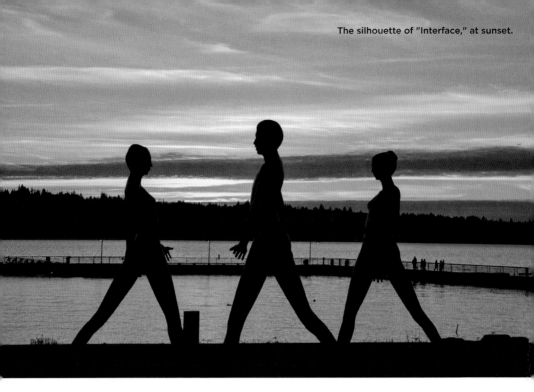

0.4   Turn left at the end of the dock.

0.5   After crossing through the boat launch area, turn left to follow the path along the shoreline.

0.6   Reach the covered picnic area and restaurants. Turn left to walk along the floating picnic dock.

0.8   At a junction with the paved path, turn left to continue walking north along the shoreline.

1.5   Reach the end of the park trail and turn around.

2.2   Back at the floating picnic dock junction, head south (left) to walk by the "Interface" art installation. Then proceed south through the covered picnic area to rejoin the main path. Return the way you came.

LOCAL INTEREST

Ivar's Seafood Bar: Enjoy fish and chips or a cup of Ivar's famous clam chowder at this waterfront location inside the park. Address: 1201 Lake Washington Blvd. N, Renton, WA; Phone: (425) 226-2122; Web: www.ivars.com

LODGING

Hyatt Regency Lake Washington: Located on the shores of Lake Washington adjacent to Gene Coulon Park. Address: 1053 Lake Washington Blvd. N, Renton, WA; Phone: (425) 203-1234; Web: www.hyatt.com

SOUTH PUGET SOUND AND SOUTHWEST WASHINGTON

South of Puget Sound and the Seattle area, several major cities thrive along the I-5 corridor. Nearest to Seattle is Tacoma, whose ongoing revitalization projects are transforming what was once an industrial area into an attractive, family friendly waterfront with miles of scenic walking paths. Tacoma's lower cost of living, relative ease of getting around, and impressive Puget Sound views have enticed many a Seattleite to move there in recent years. Take a walk from the newly restored Dune Peninsula to Point Defiance Park and perhaps you'll understand why.

The state capital of Olympia offers an eclectic mix of college-town youthfulness and capital city culture. Politicians, students, and all manner of folks can be found frequenting Olympia's crunchy cafes and eateries, forward-thinking breweries, and of course its plentiful urban green spaces. Located at the southernmost stretch of Puget Sound, this waterside city is home to perhaps the most iconic urban trail in Washington: a loop

The capitol dome on the Legislative Building is an iconic landmark for many Washingtonians.

around Capitol Lake, followed by a visit to the state capital campus. Just outside of town in neighboring Lacey, the Billy Frank Jr. Nisqually National Wildlife Refuge offers boardwalk access to a unique tidal flat estuary where diverse populations of birds and beasts make their home.

Further south along I-5, enter Southwest Washington. The star of the show here is the mighty Columbia River, which separates Washington from Oregon as it flows west to the ocean. Walk along the river on the ever-improving Columbia River Renaissance Trail in Vancouver (USA, not Canada), where a recent waterfront park overhaul is drawing visitors from across the region. At the park's showpiece, Grant Street Pier, you can walk 90 feet out over the largest river in the Pacific Northwest.

22 DUNE PENINSULA TO POINT DEFIANCE PARK

Take a waterfront stroll from Tacoma's redeveloped Dune Peninsula Park to pedestrian bridge views high above Puget Sound. Then glide back down to the marina on a series of slides before exploring the city's finest park, Point Defiance.

Elevation gain: 250 feet
Distance: 2.6-mile lollipop
Hiking time: 2 hours
Difficulty: Easy
Seasons: Year round
Trail surface: Paved path, gravel path
Land status: City park
Nearest town: Tacoma
Other users: Cyclists, joggers
Water availability: Yes, at restrooms

Canine compatibility: Dogs must remain on leash
Fees and permits: None
Map: Metro Parks Tacoma - Five Mile Drive and Trails: www.metroparkstacoma.org/five-mile-drive-trails-point-defiance
Trail contact: Metro Parks Tacoma: (253) 305-1030
Trailhead GPS: N47.3052 W122.5092

FINDING THE TRAILHEAD

From I-5, take exit 133 for I-705 North. Drive 1 mile, then use the left lane to take the Schuster Parkway exit. Follow Schuster Parkway for 1.3 miles, then make a slight left onto Ruston Way. Drive 2.9 miles. At the first traffic circle, continue straight to stay on Ruston Way. At the second traffic circle, take the 1st exit onto Yacht Club Road. Drive 0.3 miles, then turn left. Drive along the Dune Peninsula for 0.2 miles to the large parking area. Walk north from the parking area to the restrooms and trailhead.

WHAT TO SEE

Named after former Tacoma resident Frank Herbert's classic sci-fi novel, *Dune*, the Dune Peninsula at Point Defiance Park offers 11 acres of scenic saltwater shoreline for walking, cycling, and picnicking. Combine a trip to Dune Peninsula with a walk across Tacoma's newly constructed Wilson Way pedestrian bridge—a 605-foot-long, 50-foot-tall structure linking Point Defiance Park and Dune Peninsula to the Ruston Way Waterfront. If you haven't visited Tacoma in recent years, this chain of city parks connected by waterfront walkways is well worth an afternoon (or more) of exploration.

Beginning from the shaded restroom pavilion at Dune Peninsula Park, head first for the peninsula's hilltop overlook to get the lay of the land. From here you're rewarded with wide open views of ferries and sailboats on the water, while electric scooters, skateboards, and bikes cruise by below. Look south across the marina to see the Wilson Way Bridge and a series of slides descending from it—a major attraction on this urban hike. Views to the north span from the Kitsap Peninsula to Vashon and Maury Islands; Mount Rainier appears to the east in clear conditions. Kids can roll down the grassy hillside. It's incredible to consider that this peaceful park was once a smelter site whose 400,000 cubic yards of contaminated soil are now capped underfoot.

Despite decades of pollution, cleanup in recent years has allowed nature—and the public—to reclaim Dune Peninsula. Watch for seals bobbing offshore and lounging lazily

The view from Dune Peninsula on the Frank Herbert Trail as a ferry embarks.

A series of stairs and slides connects the Wilson Way Bridge to the waterfront below.

on breakwater rocks. When you reach the south end of the peninsula you have a choice: continue south to Point Ruston for access to restaurants and miles of waterfront walking. Or head west, climbing a wide path up to the Wilson Way Bridge. We suggest the Wilson Way route, but both options are worth the walk.

After 1 mile of walking from Dune Peninsula you'll reach the Wilson Way Bridge and its iconic slides. Known locally as a "chutes and ladders" experience, this series of six slides drops about 50 feet to the marina below. For kids (and many adults), it's reason enough to revisit Tacoma—especially if you're looking for a workout on the slide-side stairs. At midspan, the bridge provides a scenic overlook with views of the Vashon Island ferry, Dune Peninsula, and the slide slope. Those who wish to experience the slides without a long walk can park below the Wilson Way Bridge, near the marina.

After crossing Wilson Way Bridge, you'll enter Point Defiance Park. Opportunities for extending your hike in this 760-acre park are endless (see Going Further). Point Defiance is the crown jewel of Tacoma Metro Parks' public lands—as vital to the city as Seattle's Discovery Park or Portland's Forest Park. We suggest a short loop through the park's botanical gardens. Abloom with roses, dahlias, fuschia, and more in the summertime, these lovely gated gardens are free to enter and enjoy. Just be sure to stay on the gravel paths. The nearby Point Defiance Visitor Center is worth a stop as well, especially if you plan on extending your hike further into the park. Pick up a map here to assist with navigation. Finally, check out the peaceful Japanese Garden and pagoda before returning the way you came via Wilson Way Bridge.

Going Further: From the botanical and Japanese gardens at Point Defiance Park, you can continue west (around the zoo) for access to miles of trails. One popular route is the Spine Trail, which begins at the Rhododendron Garden and runs 2.6 miles northwest

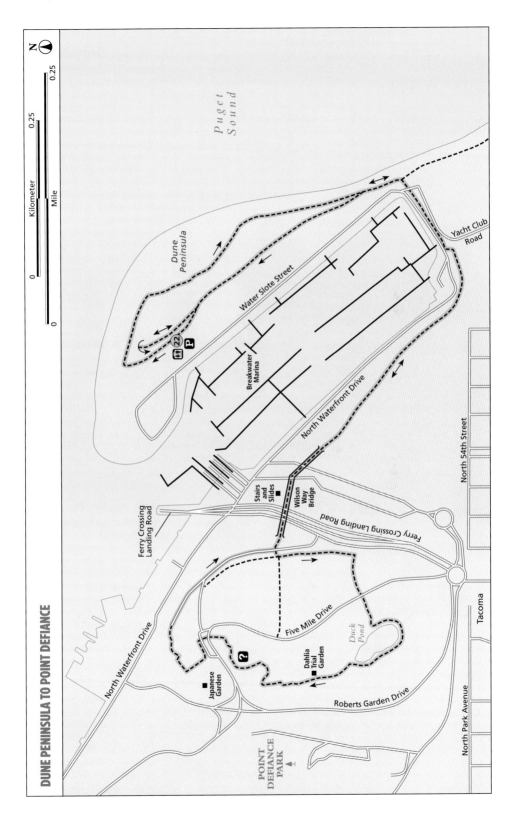

DUNE PENINSULA TO POINT DEFIANCE

N

Kilometer
0   0.25   0.25

Mile
0

Puget Sound

Dune Peninsula

Water Slote Street

Breakwater Marina

North Waterfront Drive

Yacht Club Road

Ferry Crossing Landing Road

Stairs and Slides

Wilson Way Bridge

Ferry Crossing Landing Road

North 54th Street

North Waterfront Drive

Five Mile Drive

Duck Pond

Japanese Garden

Dahlia Trial Garden

Roberts Garden Drive

North Park Avenue

Tacoma

POINT DEFIANCE PARK

The experimental flower garden in Point Defiance Park is a must-see summer highlight.

through the middle of the park. At the end, you're rewarded with a nice view of Gig Harbor across Puget Sound.

MILES AND DIRECTIONS

0.0 Beginning from the restrooms pavilion, walk northwest to ascend the small hill to an overlook.

0.1 Reach the overlook and walk back down the hill.

0.2 Turn right to walk around the peninsula, then continue south on the Frank Herbert Trail.

0.7 Turn right, cross the street, and walk beside the marina to access the Wilson Way Bridge.

1.0 Reach the slides and Wilson Way Bridge. Slide if you wish, then continue across the bridge.

1.2 Enter Point Defiance Park and turn left on the gravel Trolley Lane Trail.

1.3 Turn right, then cross Five Mile Drive and reach the duck pond.

1.4 At the duck pond turn left to walk around the pond. Then continue north through the botanical gardens.

1.6 Exit the botanical gardens, and walk north to reach the visitor center. Then cross Five Mile Drive to reach the Japanese Gardens and pagoda.

1.7 Walk clockwise around the pagoda, entering the Japanese Gardens if you wish. Then turn east to take the Trolley Lane Trail south to Wilson Way Bridge. Retrace your steps to Dune Peninsula.

LOCAL INTEREST

Point Defiance Zoo & Aquarium: Established in 1905, Point Defiance is the only combined zoo and aquarium in the Pacific Northwest. Discover hundreds of species at this 29-acre zoo located inside Point Defiance Park. Address: 5400 N Pearl St., Tacoma, WA; Phone: (253) 404-3800; Web: www.pdza.org

Point Ruston: Connecting Dune Peninsula and Point Defiance to downtown Tacoma, Point Ruston is your nearest stop for food and drinks. Walk south from Dune Peninsula along the Ruston Way Waterfront for access to restaurants and the Point Ruston farmers market (held Sundays during summer). Address: 5005 Ruston Way, Tacoma, WA; Web: www.pointruston.com

LODGING

McMenamins Elks Temple: With seven floors of bars, guestrooms and restaurants, this restored 1916 building is once again a hotspot in downtown Tacoma. Stop by for a drink on the Spanish Steps, or spend the night exploring! Can you find the secret bar? Address: 565 Broadway, Tacoma, WA; Phone: (425) 219-4370; Web: www.mcmenamins.com/elks-temple

23 BILLY FRANK JR. NISQUALLY NATIONAL WILDLIFE REFUGE

Explore one of the last remaining tidal flat estuaries in the Puget Sound, with the chance to spot countless types of wildlife from a unique elevated boardwalk trail system.

Elevation gain: Minimal
Distance: 4.4 miles out-and-back
Hiking time: 2 hours
Difficulty: Easy
Seasons: Year round
Trail surface: Boardwalk, gravel path, paved path
Land status: National wildlife refuge
Nearest town: Lacey
Other users: None (cycling and jogging prohibited)
Water availability: Yes, at restrooms

Canine compatibility: Dogs prohibited
Fees and permits: $3 daily fee per four adults. Interagency passes are accepted.
Map: Refuge Trail Map - Billy Frank Jr. Nisqually National Wildlife Refuge: www.fws.gov/refuge/Billy_Frank_Jr_Nisqually/map.html
Trail contact: US Fish and Wildlife Service: (360) 753-9467
Trailhead GPS: N47.0728 W122.7129

FINDING THE TRAILHEAD

From I-5, take Exit 114 toward Nisqually. After exiting the freeway, head north on Brown Farm Roadd NE and turn right to stay on Brown Farm Road. Drive 0.6 miles to a large parking lot. Cross the parking lot and begin your hike from the kiosk outside the visitor center.

WHAT TO SEE

Teeming with wildlife, Billy Frank Jr. Nisqually National Wildlife Refuge is ideal for a leg stretch right off of the I-5 corridor between Tacoma and Olympia. One of the few remaining major estuaries in the Puget Sound not encroached upon by human industry, the Nisqually Delta is imperative for migratory birds, fish, and other endangered species. A chance to observe this unique habitat and wildlife is accessible from a network of elevated boardwalks and trails.

From the visitor's center, head clockwise on the Twin Barns Loop that extends from either side of the trailhead kiosk. Before setting out, make sure you pay the entrance fee using the envelopes provided, and pick up a trail map. The path soon transitions to a boardwalk, elevated above the wetlands below. Birds twitter in the trees, and you might catch sight of a beaver, or the red-brown Northern red-legged frog. Cottonwood and alder trees offer areas of green–filtered shade, making the area a pleasant oasis even on the hottest summer days.

Turn off onto the Twin Barns observation platform for a view of the structures that give this loop its name. The pale-colored buildings are all that remains of the Brown family's former dairy farm. In the early 1900s the Brown family built a large dike to leach out salt from the river delta to create pasture land. Unfortunately, this led to the destruction of important habitat for salmon, making their transition from ocean living to

Be on the lookout for Great Blue Herons who commonly make their home in the Nisqually estuary.

Explore the Nisqually estuary on a raised boardwalk for views of tidal flats and the Puget Sound.

freshwater spawning grounds. Although the wildlife refuge was established in 1974, the area was not fully restored until 2009 when the dikes were removed.

When you head back towards the Twin Barns Loop, instead of returning to the board-walk, turn left and start out on the Nisqually Estuary Trail. As it extends out over the tidal flats of the river delta, the landscape around this trail is in constant flux. High tide or low tide, summer or winter—each has its own appeal. In the winter, the river runs high, flooding the flats. In the summer, herons dot the shores teaching their fledglings to hunt on their own alongside gulls and other shorebirds. The highlight of the refuge, the elevated boardwalk offers a spectacular view out to Puget Sound. Be mindful: with the exception of three covered areas, the full mile of boardwalk is exposed to the elements.

At the end of the boardwalk (the last 0.1 mile is closed October through January for hunting season) you'll be greeted with a beautiful view of the river meeting the sea. In the distance you'll spy the Tacoma Narrows Bridge, and in front of you is Anderson Island and the Key Peninsula. Make sure you take the time to look through the viewing scope on this platform. You never know what might be wading through the waves in the distance!

Head back along the boardwalk and rejoin up with the Twin Barns Loop, heading towards the visitor center. After the long exposed trail through the estuary, you may be thankful for the tree cover here. Along this stretch of trail there are two optional side trails out to different viewing areas. One leads to a view of the Nisqually River, and the second focuses on riparian forests.

And perhaps you've been wondering: who is Billy Frank Jr.? A tireless activist and founder of the Northwest Indian Fisheries Commission, Billy Frank Jr. fought against the threat of industrial takeover of the Nisqually Delta. As a vocal member of the Nisqually tribe, he used good old civil disobedience in order to petition the government to uphold

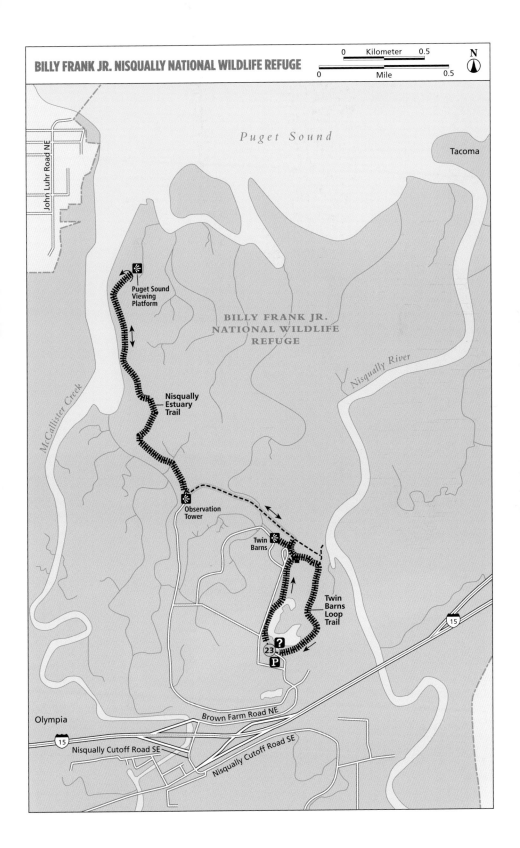

BILLY FRANK JR. NISQUALLY NATIONAL WILDLIFE REFUGE

0   Kilometer   0.5

0   Mile   0.5

N

Puget Sound

Tacoma

John Luhr Road NE

Puget Sound Viewing Platform

BILLY FRANK JR.
NATIONAL WILDLIFE
REFUGE

Nisqually River

Nisqually Estuary Trail

McCallister Creek

Observation Tower

Twin Barns

Twin Barns Loop Trail

15

23

P

Olympia

Brown Farm Road NE

15

Nisqually Cutoff Road SE

Nisqually Cutoff Road SE

The Twin Barns are a reminder of the Brown Farm, which once occupied the Nisqually River Delta. Today, much of the delta has been reclaimed for the estuary ecosystem.

the stipulations of the Medicine Creek Treaty. In honoring Nisqually fishing rights, the estuary was preserved for future generations, and now bears the name of the man who fought to save it.

MILES AND DIRECTIONS

0.0   From the visitor center kiosk, walk northwest on the sidewalk to access the Twin Barns Loop Trail.

0.1   Continue straight at the junction onto a boardwalk.

0.5   Turn left, then continue straight through a second intersection to reach the Twin Barns Observation Platform.

0.6   Reach the observation platform, then retrace your steps to the previous intersection. Turn left, then left again onto the gravel Nisqually Estuary Trail.

1.1   Turn right onto the boardwalk. You can access another observation tower here.

1.5   Reach the Medicine Creek Viewing Platform. Continue north on the boardwalk.

2.1   Reach a seasonal gate, closed early October through late January. Proceed if the gate is open.

2.2   Reach the Puget Sound Viewing Platform. Turn around and retrace your steps to the Twin Barns Observation Platform trail intersection.

3.8   Turn right, then turn left onto the Twin Barns Loop Trail. Follow the loop south, returning to the visitor center.

LOCAL INTEREST

Top Rung Brewing: A lively neighborhood brewery, Top Rung was founded by two firefighters with a love of craft beer. Address: 8343 Hogum Bay Ln. NE, Lacey, WA; Phone: (360) 915-8766; Web: www.toprungbrewing.com/

LODGING

Best Western Plus Lacey Inn & Suites: Clean, modern rooms, convenient location near Nisqually NWR, and a continental breakfast make Best Western Plus a great basecamp for your South Sound adventures. Address: 8326 Quinault Dr. NE, Lacey, WA; Phone: (360) 456-5655; Web: www.bestwestern.com

24 CAPITOL LAKE LOOP

Visit Washington State's capital and explore a scene torn right from a postcard: the iconic Legislative Building reflected in the placid waters of Capitol Lake.

Elevation gain: 115 feet
Distance: 2.5-mile loop
Hiking time: 1 hour
Difficulty: Easy
Seasons: Year round
Trail surface: Paved path, gravel
Land status: State land
Nearest town: Olympia
Other users: Joggers
Water availability: Yes, at restrooms

Canine compatibility: Dogs must remain on leash
Fees and permits: None (free parking limited to 2 hours)
Map: Washington State Department of Enterprise Services - Capitol Lake Trails: www.des.wa.gov/
Trail contact: Washington State Department of Enterprise Services: (360) 902-8880
Trailhead GPS: N47.0367 W122.9122

FINDING THE TRAILHEAD

From I-5, take exit 105 toward Port of Olympia. Continue north onto Plum Street SE for 0.5 mile. Turn left onto 5th Avenue SE and drive 0.8 mile. Make a slight left onto Deschutes Parkway SW, then drive 0.6 mile. Turn left into Marathon Park. Begin your walk near the restrooms, heading north on the sidewalk for a clockwise loop.

WHAT TO SEE

The salt air tickles your nose as you round the still waters of the lake; a reflection of the stately sandstone dome is broken only by an incoming great blue heron. This is the scene awaiting you on your hike at Capitol Lake in Olympia. The 1.5-mile loop around the lake offers stunning views of the Legislative Building's neoclassical architecture as well as views towards downtown Olympia and Budd Inlet.

Start from Marathon Park to head clockwise along the wide paved sidewalk. This section of trail runs alongside the busy Deschutes Parkway so be prepared for road noise. Along the shores though, you'll be able to spot herons and other waterfowl as they plod through the shallows. Capitol Lake is an artificial lake, part of the master plan design of the Capitol Campus designed by New York architects Wilder and White. It was formerly an estuary at the mouth of the Deschutes River (known best for Tumwater Falls and the site of the famed Olympia Brewery).

The lake was once a recreation playground, but closed in 2009 to swimming and boating. An infestation of New Zealand mud snails—a non-native and highly invasive pest—is the foremost reason for the closure. For over a decade, plans to return the lake to its former estuary glory have been on the table. But nature is already gaining headway: during our visit we not only spotted a host of birds, but also multiple frogs and even a river otter.

At the northern end of the lake, you'll enter into Heritage Park. The highlight along this stretch are plaques honoring all of Washington State's counties. Young Washingtonians will enjoy finding their home county. At 1.1 miles from the trailhead, you'll reach

A side trail gently switchbacks up the hillside to the Capitol Campus.

Capitol Lake and the Olympia waterfront as seen from the Capitol Campus above.

the Heritage Park Trail, which switchbacks up the bluff to the Capitol Campus above. The grade is easily managed, but the trail is fully exposed and can feel unforgiving in mid-summer heat. The view from the top is worth it in any condition. On crisp winter days, you'll be able to gaze out upon the snowcapped Olympic Mountains rising from the waters of Puget Sound.

Washington State's Capitol Campus is worthy of a full day of exploration, but this route takes you past the two most impressive buildings: the Temple of Justice and Legislative Building. The Temple of Justice features a formidable wall of Corinthian columns. Taken on its own, this sandstone structure would be an architectural giant. Instead, it demures to the majesty of the Legislative Building. Featuring the tallest self-supported stone dome in North America at 287 feet, it's the image that comes to mind for many Washingtonians when they picture the capital. If time allows, explore both buildings which are open to the public and offer tours. See visitor information below for hours and contact info.

After making a loop around the Temple of Justice, head back down the Heritage Park Trail to meet back up with the Capitol Lake Trail. This section of trail is a bit more manicured, with benches, lake overlooks, and landscaped trees. Continue on this trail over a bridge that connects back to Marathon Park. As you head back to your car, imagine the possibilities of how Capitol Lake may change in the future.

Going Further: From Marathon Park, you could continue on the trail to an Interpretive Center at the southern end of the lake. From there it's possible to continue on to Tumwater Historical Park and Brewery Park at Tumwater Falls.

CAPITOL LAKE TRAIL

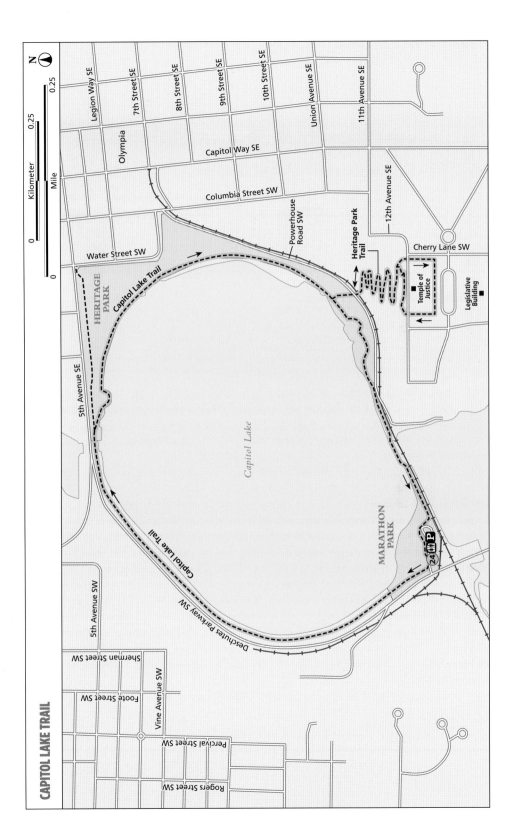

- Legion Way SE
- 7th Street SE
- 8th Street SE
- 9th Street SE
- 10th Street SE
- Union Avenue SE
- 11th Avenue SE
- Olympia
- Capitol Way SE
- Columbia Street SW
- Powerhouse Road SW
- 12th Avenue SE
- Heritage Park Trail
- Cherry Lane SW
- Temple of Justice
- Legislative Building
- Water Street SW
- HERITAGE PARK
- Capitol Lake Trail
- 5th Avenue SE
- Capitol Lake
- Capitol Lake Trail
- Deschutes Parkway SW
- MARATHON PARK
- 5th Avenue SW
- Sherman Street SW
- Foote Street SW
- Vine Avenue SW
- Percival Street SW
- Rogers Street SW

N

Kilometer
0   0.25   0.25

Mile
0

A heron rests on a set of buoys in Capitol Lake. Capitol Lake itself has been closed in recent years due to many ecological disturbances.

MILES AND DIRECTIONS

0.0 From the restrooms at Marathon Park, walk north on the sidewalk along Deschutes Parkway.

0.6 Cross Deschutes Dam and turn right to follow the path around Capitol Lake.

1.1 Turn left and cross the tracks. Then climb the switchbacks to the capitol campus.

1.5 Reach the end of the switchbacks and cross 12th Avenue, walking south on the sidewalk. Then turn right to walk between the Legislative Building and Temple of Justice.

1.6 Turn right (north) to loop back to the switchbacks. Walk through the Law Enforcement Memorial, then descend the switchbacks to the loop trail below.

2.1 Turn left on the Capitol Lake Loop and return to Marathon Park.

LOCAL INTEREST

Legislative Building Tours: Free, guided public tours of the Washington State Capitol Building are available daily. Address: 416 Sid Snyder Ave. SW, Olympia, WA; Phone: (360) 902-8880; Web: www.des.wa.gov/services/facilities-leasing/capitol-campus/tours

Brewery Park at Tumwater Falls: Visit famed Tumwater Falls and get your fill of Washington State brewing history. Another great place for a leg stretch or picnic break. Address: 110 Deschutes Way SW, Tumwater, WA; Phone: (360) 943-2550; Web: www.olytumfoundation.org/

Well 80 Brewhouse: It's the water! Honoring the legacy of Olympia Brewing, Well 80 brews with 100 percent artesian well water in a nostalgia-tinted brewpub. Make sure to try Leopold's Lager. Address: 514 4th Ave. E, Olympia, WA; Phone: (360) 915-6653; Web: www.well80.com

LODGING

Hotel RL Olympia: Located just west of Capitol Lake, this full-service hotel features guest rooms with Olympia-inspired artwork and offers lake views. Address: 2300 Evergreen Park Dr. SW, Olympia, WA; Phone: (360) 943-4000, Web: www.redlion.com/hotelrl/olympia

25 ELLIS COVE TRAIL

Just 2 miles from downtown Olympia, a 314-acre nature park sits peacefully on the shores of Budd Inlet. Hike Ellis Cove Trail for beach access, city views, and a surprisingly lush forest-bathing experience at Priest Point Park.

Elevation gain: 350 feet
Distance: 2.3-mile lollipop
Hiking time: 1–2 hours
Difficulty: Moderate
Seasons: Year round
Trail surface: Dirt path, boardwalk
Land status: City park
Nearest town: Olympia
Other users: Joggers (bikes prohibited)
Water availability: Yes, at restrooms

Canine compatibility: Dogs must remain on leash
Fees and permits: None
Map: Priest Point Park Map - City of Olympia: www.olympiawa.gov/community/parks/parks-and-trails/priest-point-park
Trail contact: City of Olympia Parks: (360) 753-8380
Trailhead GPS: N47.0714 W122.8950

FINDING THE TRAILHEAD

From I-5, take exit 105 toward Port of Olympia. Continue north onto Plum Street SE for 0.6 miles. Continue onto East Bay Drive NE for 1.5 miles, then turn right into Priest Point Park. Drive 0.2 miles, passing the rose garden, and turn left to cross a bridge. At the end of the bridge turn right and park in the designated spaces. To find the trailhead, walk north from the parking lot to East Bay Drive NE. Then walk north along the road for 200 feet, where you'll find the trailhead kiosk on the left.

WHAT TO SEE

Urban hikers, birders, and escapists rejoice. On the fringe of Washington State's capital city, an outdoor oasis awaits. For hikers, over 4 miles of trails crisscross Priest Point Park. Birders will find bald eagles, osprey, great blue herons, and kingfishers. And if you're simply looking for an escape from the city, Priest Point is hard to beat. In less than 1 mile of walking you'll be looking back on Olympia shimmering in the distance—so close, yet seemingly so far away. Ellis Cove Trail ranks among Washington's most rewarding urban hikes.

The best way to access Priest Point Park's 1 mile of saltwater shoreline is via Ellis Cove Trail. By walking around Ellis Cove—a finger-like extension of Budd Inlet—you can access a relatively quiet beach with views across the saltwater to downtown Olympia. Begin your hike by entering Priest Point Park's dense forest. Big leaf maples overhead and all manner of ferns below (sword, maidenhair, and licorice) create a lush, deep-forest feeling just steps from the trailhead. But you're far from neither road nor saltwater—at low tide, sea scents ride the breeze from Ellis Cove to meet you in the woods.

The trail drops quickly via steps and steep sections. You'll dip into ravines, crossing boardwalks before climbing back up again—a rollercoaster hiking (or trail running) adventure. Watch for moss-covered animal figures in the trees (there's at least one bear up there!). When you reach the loop junction at 0.6 miles (marked by another furry

A madrone tree reaches out from the bluff towards Budd Inlet.

Take a side trail down to the beach to experience Ellis Cove and the Budd Inlet.

friend), bear left for a clockwise loop. By sticking to the shoreline, you'll gain access to the beach in no time. The first beach opportunity comes at 0.8 miles, but hiking further out is more rewarding. From a bluff-top overlook at the south end of Priest Point, twisted madrone trees reach southward towards the Capitol Building. Take a moment here to remember how close you are to the city.

For its relatively small size, Priest Point Park feels vast and sprawling. Enjoy peek-a-boo water views as you continue north and finally reach the beach. Then spend some time strolling along the pebble-strewn shoreline before returning to the trailhead via the loop. Finally, be sure to stop by the park's rose garden—located on the east side of East Bay Drive NE—on your way out. Gardens were first planted here by Catholic missionaries in 1848 before the city acquired the land in 1905. The park became known as Priest Point due to its history as a mission. Yet before settlers arrived, indigenous peoples had long occupied the land. Over a century later, the gardens, well-preserved forest, and name are a reminder of this land's timeless place in Washington State history.

MILES AND DIRECTIONS

0.0   From the trailhead kiosk, walk west on Ellis Cove Trail.

0.3   Turn left to stay on Ellis Cove Trail

0.6   Reach the loop. Turn left to hike in a clockwise direction.

0.8   Stay right at the junction. The trail to the left descends to the beach.

1.0   Turn left here and at the next two junctions.

1.3   Turn left for beach access. Then return to this junction and retrace your steps back to the loop trail.

The trail crosses multiple boardwalk bridges, shaded by the expansive canopy above.

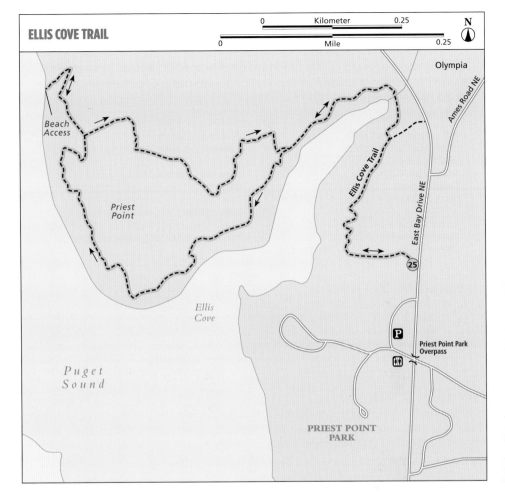

ELLIS COVE TRAIL

0	Kilometer	0.25
0	Mile	0.25

N

Olympia

Beach Access

Priest Point

Ellis Cove Trail

East Bay Drive NE

Ames Road NE

25

Ellis Cove

Puget Sound

P

Priest Point Park Overpass

PRIEST POINT PARK

1.5   Turn left.

1.6   Continue straight through the junction.

1.8   Finish the loop and retrace your steps to the trailhead.

LOCAL INTEREST

Three Magnets Brewing: Experimental brewery known for its hazy IPAs and small-batch farmhouse ales. Their family friendly restaurant serves excellent, locally sourced foods. Address: 600 Franklin St. SE #105, Olympia, WA; Phone: (360) 972-2481; Web: www.threemagnetsbrewing.com

LODGING

Best Western Plus Lacey Inn & Suites: Clean, modern rooms and continental breakfast make Best Western Plus a great basecamp for your South Sound adventures. Address: 8326 Quinault Dr. NE, Lacey, WA; Phone: (360) 456-5655; Web: www.bestwestern.com

26 LAKE SACAJAWEA PARK

Take a walk around Lake Sacajawea Park Arboretum and explore everything from a solar system walk to Japanese Gardens in the Tree City, USA of Longview.

Elevation gain: 64 feet
Distance: 4.3-mile loop
Hiking time: 2 hours
Difficulty: Easy
Seasons: Year round
Trail surface: Gravel path, paved path
Land status: City park
Nearest town: Longview
Other users: Cyclists, joggers

Water availability: Yes, at restrooms
Canine compatibility: Dogs must remain on leash
Fees and permits: None
Map: Lake Sacajawea Frank Willis Arboretum - www.mylongview.com
Trail contact: City of Longview, Parks Division: (360) 577-3345
Trailhead GPS: N46.1380 W122.9504

FINDING THE TRAILHEAD

From Vancouver, WA, take I-5 north to exit 36. Continue onto WA-432 W toward Longview. Drive 2.4 miles, then continue onto Tennant Way. Drive 1 mile, then turn right onto 15th Avenue. Take an immediate left onto E Kessler Blvd. Drive 1 mile and park on the street near the intersection with Hemlock Street. The trailhead is at a large wooden structure near the restrooms.

WHAT TO SEE

When you think of the great city parks in the United States, the first that come to mind are most likely Central Park in New York, or Golden Gate Park in San Francisco. Lake Sacajawea Park in Longview, WA, may not come to mind, but this city park offers a checklist of sights to rival the greats. The park is also an arboretum and within 4 miles of walking around this manmade lake, over 100 species of trees can be discovered.

The city of Longview was conceived (and largely funded) by Robert A. Long in the early 1920s as a planned community to support the large workforce needed for the two Long-Bell lumber mills Long wanted to build in Cowlitz County. Famed city planner George Kessler is responsible for the comprehensive city plan of Longview. As a player in the City Beautiful movement, Kessler was the initial designer of Lake Sacajawea Park, intending it to be a focal point of the city. Through the years, the park has changed with the times, shaped by the needs of the community around it.

With plenty of parking along the boulevards that surround the lake, it's possible to enter the park at virtually any point along the trail. For the purposes of this trail description, we will describe a route starting from a midpoint greenspace with a playground and restrooms. Head out on the gravel trail towards Lions Island, crossing the small footbridge to explore the island. Here you'll discover a totem pole and beautiful views down the spine of the lake. Back on the main trail, the east side of the lake parallels Kessler Boulevard, lined with schools, churches, and historic mansions, offering some solitude during your walk. At 0.9 miles, keep towards the path closest to the lake to take the pedestrian underpass beneath 20th Avenue.

Pioneer Lions Island
with water fountain
in the background.

Pedestrian bridge over
Lake Sacajawea.

The southern end of the lake, near the hospital, feels considerably more urban with the rising noise of traffic from Nichols Boulevard. But paths closer to the lake and the surrounding large oak trees maintain the natural feel of the park. At 1.3 miles, you'll come to the beginning of the Solar System Walk. Young hikers will enjoy watching for the stone plaques along the path describing the relative distances between the planets of our solar system. A small note: Pluto's plaque is still in place, offering the chance at a fun astronomical debate. You can even continue to use the pedestrian underpasses and never miss a planet.

At 2.2 miles, take the side path through a flower garden—especially fragrant in the late spring as the peonies bloom. One of the most picturesque angles in the park comes into view at 2.4 miles. Surrounded by willows, waterlilies fanning the lake's edge, the pedestrian bridge looks like something out of Monet's garden. Relax on a bench, or keep on along a long tree-lined stretch.

After rounding the north end of the lake, the entrance to the Japanese Gardens is found at 3.5 miles. A meditative path winds its way towards the entrance gate. The garden does close for the evenings, so plan your hike accordingly. If the gate is open, cross the red bridge to the island and take in the garden's tranquility. Circle back to the main path and continue on through the rhododendron gardens at 4.0 miles, ending your loop back at the trailhead at just over 4.2 miles.

MILES AND DIRECTIONS

0.0 Head south on the gravel path from the trailhead at Kaiser Boulevard and Hemlock Street.

0.2 Turn right to enter Pioneer Lions Island and walk its length. At the south end of the island, turn around and return to the main trail.

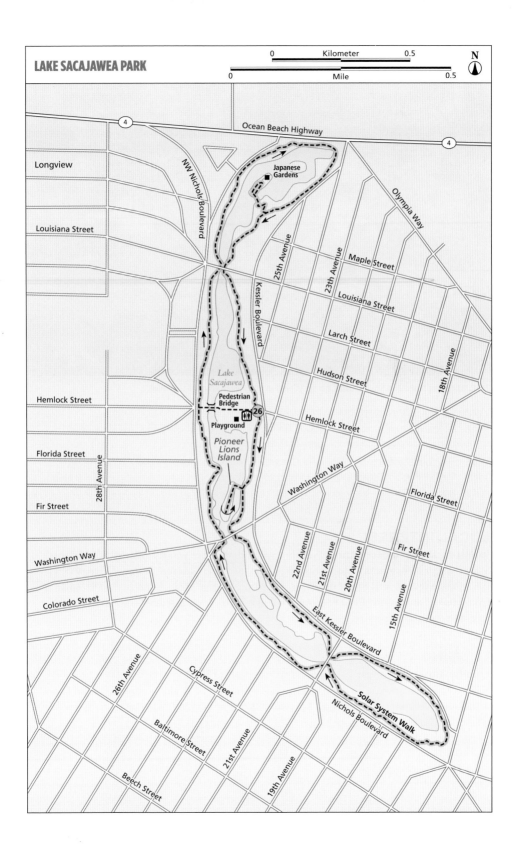

Kilometer

0   0.5

0   Mile   0.5

N

Longview

Louisiana Street

Ocean Beach Highway

NW Nichols Boulevard

Japanese Gardens

Olympia Way

25th Avenue

23rd Avenue

Maple Street

Kessler Boulevard

Louisiana Street

Larch Street

Hudson Street

18th Avenue

Lake Sacajawea

Hemlock Street

Pedestrian Bridge

Playground

26

Hemlock Street

Florida Street

Pioneer Lions Island

28th Avenue

Washington Way

Fir Street

Florida Street

Washington Way

22nd Avenue

21st Avenue

20th Avenue

Fir Street

Colorado Street

15th Avenue

East Kessler Boulevard

26th Avenue

Cypress Street

Solar System Walk

Baltimore Street

Nichols Boulevard

21st Avenue

Beech Street

19th Avenue

The Japanese Gardens are located on an island in the north end of the lake.

0.4 Continue south on the loop trail.

0.5 Reach the first of several bridges. Stay right (stick to the water) to use the pedestrian underpass and avoid crossing the street.

3.5 Turn right to enter the Japanese Gardens. Explore the gardens, then return to the main trail and continue walking south.

4.3 Reach the trailhead and conclude your urban hike.

LOCAL INTEREST

Johnston Ridge Observatory: Nothing will fully prepare you for the sight of Mount St. Helens, which is more than enough reason to visit Johnston Ridge. Learn about the 1980 eruption and how nature is returning to the area. Address: 24000 Spirit Lake Hwy, Toutle, WA; Phone: (360)274-2140; Web: www.fs.fed.us/visit/destination/johnston-ridge-observatory

LODGING

Quality Inn and Suites: Conveniently located off of the highway and close to Lake Sacajawea Park. Pet friendly, the hotel also has an indoor pool, and continental breakfast is included. Address: 723 7th Ave., Longview, WA; Phone: (360) 414-1000; Web: www.choicehotels.com/washington/longview/quality-inn-hotels

27 COLUMBIA RIVER RENAISSANCE TRAIL

Take a walk along the Columbia River, at the border between Washington and Oregon, to experience the revitalization of Vancouver's downtown waterfront.

Elevation gain: Minimal
Distance: 3.4 miles out and back
Hiking time: 2 hours
Difficulty: Easy
Seasons: Year round
Trail surface: Paved path
Land status: City park
Nearest town: Vancouver
Other users: Cyclists, joggers
Water availability: None

Canine compatibility: Dogs must remain on leash
Fees and permits: None
Map: Columbia River Renaissance Trail - City of Vancouver: www.cityofvancouver.us
Trail contact: Vancouver Parks & Recreation: (360) 487-8311
Trailhead GPS: N45.6149 W122.6527

FINDING THE TRAILHEAD

From I-5, take exit 1A for WA-14 East toward Camas. Drive 0.7 miles, then continue onto WA-14 East. Drive 0.4 miles, then use the right lane to take exit 1 for SE Columbia Way toward Vancouver National Historic Reserve. Drive 0.3 miles, then keep right, following signs for SE Columbia Shores Boulevard and merging onto SE Columbia Shores Boulevard. Drive 0.2 miles and after crossing SE Columbia River Drive, park in the ample business parking lots near McMenamins on the Columbia.

WHAT TO SEE

Vancouver, Washington is undergoing a revamp: its renovated waterfront district is a new dining hotspot, honoring the Columbia River it borders. The Columbia River Renaissance Trail offers a walk through the heart of the revitalization, with the constant rolling of the mighty Columbia as its backdrop. End your urban hike with happy hour at one of Vancouver's newest waterfront bars or restaurants.

Setting off from the eastern end of the trail in the Columbia Shores business complex, river views are instantaneous. Look across the waters to the shores of Oregon, and watch for all manner of boats and ships. Round the corner of the business park and you'll come to Surprise Beach. There is access to the beach here, if you need to dip your toes on warm summer days. From here, the trail veers away from the shoreline, following Columbia Way for a short time on a wide tree-lined sidewalk.

After a bit of road-side trail walking, a green space allows you to get back to those excellent river views as a paved trail diverts from the sidewalk. The Columbia River Renaissance Trail and much of the green space on this stretch is part of the Fort Vancouver National Historic Site. A land bridge connects the trail to Fort Vancouver, offering even more options for exploration.

At the end of this pocket park (1 mile from the trailhead), you'll come to a large parking lot. At the time of research and writing, this section of the waterfront redevelopment was in flux. There are plans to continue the trail along the river, but no firm timeline is

A young cottontail rabbit as seen along the waterfront trail.

in place for changes. Return to the sidewalk along this stretch to cross under I-5 and pass the Captain George Vancouver Monument. Continue along the sidewalk past the Port of Vancouver Terminal 1 (another area that will be renovated in the years to come). You may have to assess the best way through the ongoing construction, but sidewalks should be in place to help with navigation. Follow the riverfront west to find your way.

Welcome to the Vancouver Waterfront! The lush Waterfront Park blends seamlessly into the restaurant and retail spaces of the new development. And from here, you'll see the jewel of this project: the Grant Street Pier. Wander through the park, and make sure to check out the interactive Headwaters Wall, which honors the Columbia River watershed. Then head to the pier! Like a modern art take on a mast and sail, the Grant Street Pier juts 90 feet out over the Columbia River. Illuminated at night, the pier is a great spot to catch the sunset, or do a little stargazing. Return the way you came, and see if anything else has changed in the meantime!

Going Further: Miles of trails are available at Fort Vancouver, which can be accessed via a land bridge found across Columbia Way just east of I-5. Make sure to keep a lookout for the old apple tree, said to be the oldest apple tree in Washington State. Fort Vancouver also provides an alternative starting point for this urban hike, with plenty of parking available.

MILES AND DIRECTIONS

0.0 From the trailhead on the east side of McMenamins on the Columbia, take the ramp down to the waterfront trail and head west.

0.4 The trail meets Southeast Columbia Way. Continue west on the wide sidewalk path.

0.8 Turn left into road-side park, following the trail along the river shoreline.

The Grant Street Pier is a highlight of Vancouver's new urban plaza.

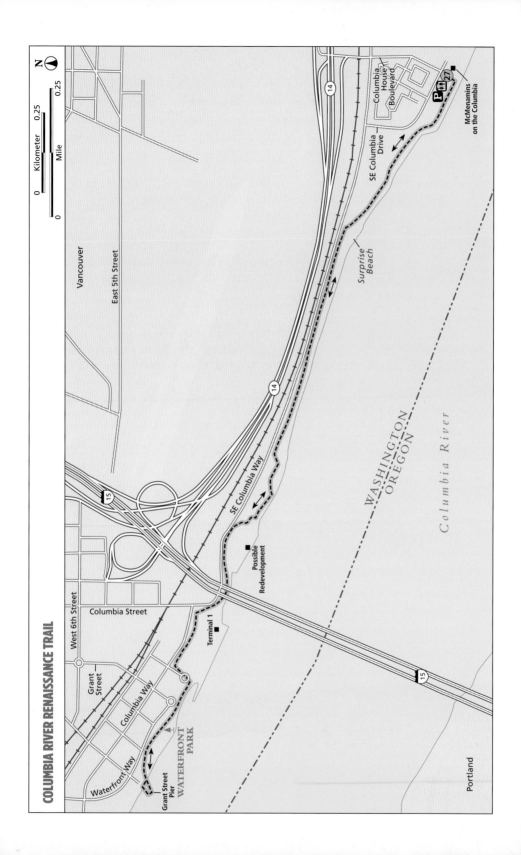

COLUMBIA RIVER RENAISSANCE TRAIL

N

0 0.25 Kilometer
0 0.25 Mile

Vancouver

West 6th Street

Columbia Street

Grant Street

Columbia Way

Waterfront Way

Grant Street Pier

WATERFRONT PARK

East 5th Street

Terminal 1

Possible Redevelopment

SE Columbia Way

14

15

WASHINGTON
OREGON

Columbia River

Surprise Beach

SE Columbia Drive

Columbia House Boulevard

14

P 🛈 27

McMenamins on the Columbia

15

Portland

1.0	Rejoin the wide sidewalk path, following the trail west as it continues around businesses.
1.3	After passing under the bridges, head left on the sidewalk along Columbia Way.
1.4	Turn left to access Vancouver Landing. Then continue west along the waterfront.
1.7	Reach Grant Street Pier. Retrace your steps to the trailhead.

LOCAL INTEREST

Fort Vancouver: Historic homes, air museum, and the story of the Pacific Northwest await at this National Historic Site. Address: 612 E Reserve St., Vancouver, WA; Phone: (360) 816-6230; Web: www.nps.gov/fova/index.htm

Maryhill Winery Vancouver Tasting Room: Based upriver on the Columbia in Goldendale, Maryhill is one of Washington's favorite wineries. Sip their world-class wines with a view of Grant Street Pier and the Columbia River. Address: 801 Waterfront Way Ste. 105, Vancouver, WA; Phone: (360) 450-6211; Web: www.maryhillwinery.com

LODGING

Hilton Vancouver Washington: Full-service hotel with park-view suites in Downtown Vancouver. Located across the street from Esther Short Park and Loowit Brewing, this hotel's central location can't be beat. Address: 301 W 6th St, Vancouver, WA; Phone: (360) 993-4500; Web: www.3hilton.com

28 ROUND LAKE LOOP

Great for getting outdoors during winter, lily-spotting in the spring, summer swimming and fall colors, this little lake is the perfect urban escape any time of year. Hike this short loop to experience Round Lake's many unique charms.

Elevation gain: 250 feet
Distance: 2.2-mile loop
Hiking time: 1-2 hours
Difficulty: Moderate
Seasons: Year round
Trail surface: Gravel path, paved path, dirt path
Land status: County Park
Nearest town: Camas
Other users: Joggers, cyclists

Water availability: Yes, at restrooms
Canine compatibility: Dogs must remain on leash
Fees and permits: None
Map: City of Camas Trails Map - www .cityofcamas.us
Trail contact: Clark County Parks: (360) 397-2285
Trailhead GPS: N45.6040 W122.4070

FINDING THE TRAILHEAD

From Vancouver, take WA-14 E toward Camas. Take exit 12 for Camas and continue 0.4 mile to a traffic circle. At the traffic circle, take the 2nd exit onto NW 6th Avenue. Drive 1.3 miles, then turn left onto NE Garfield Street. NE Garfield Street turns slightly left and becomes NE 14th Avenue. Drive 0.1 miles then turn right onto WA-500 W/NE Everett Street. Drive 1 mile, then turn right into the Lacamas Park parking lot. The trail begins at the north end of the lot. Additional parking is available on the north side of NE 35th Avenue.

WHAT TO SEE

A summer hotspot just north of Camas, Round Lake at Lacamas Park is open year round for hiking, swimming, paddling and fishing. The small parking lot fills up quickly for good reason: it's an easy getaway from the city, with waterfalls and wildflowers to boot. Begin your hike from the busy lakeside picnic area at Lacamas Park. Here you'll find access to restrooms and water, a playground, and paved paths leading to well-shaded picnic spots. You can also read up on the park's history and grab an interpretive trail guide at the park kiosk. When you're ready to hit the trail, head north over a sturdy pedestrian bridge. To your left, 296-acre Lacamas Lake flows into 26-acre Round Lake on your right.

Hiking this loop in a clockwise direction allows users to get the not-so-scenic part out of the way first. Namely, a short section of road-walking along a fenceline. Once you hit gravel after 0.2 miles though, you'll forget about the pavement as you descend gently into treecover. The trail is easygoing for the first 0.5 miles, leading to a viewing platform with open lake views. The pace picks up from here, as the trail gains 200 feet of elevation over the next 0.5 miles. Take a rest at a well-placed bench among the big leaf maple and hemlock trees, peering down on the lake below.

When you reach the 0.7-mile mark, head left for the Camas Lily Loop if visiting during bloom season (usually mid-April). Alternatively, you can stay on the Round Lake Loop for a shorter hike. Signage at Lacamas Park can be somewhat confusing, so follow

The dam at Lacamas Creek empties into Pothole Falls.

our Miles and Directions when in doubt. The Lily Trail heads north, climbing through forest and meadow to a high point of 400 feet at 1 mile. Along the way you can see lovely violet-hued camas lilies that the city of Camas is named after. The trail drops as you round the Lily Loop, making its way back to Round Lake.

At 1.6 miles, a mess of trails converge. Head left here for the fenceline at Pothole Falls overlook.

Swift waters carry loose rocks along Lacamas Creek, grinding them into the soft bedrock here to create the "potholes." During summer, the pockmarked pools are a popular swimming spot. Continuing north, reach the dam and cross it for views of Round Lake's waters cascading down into Lacamas Creek. Then cross the fish screen, which helps prevent fish and debris from entering the Mill Pond west of Round Lake.

The final stretch of trail is flat, wide and easy between the dams and the picnic area. Soon, you'll start seeing picnic tables in the trees and hit the pavement again before you know it. If you've brought lunch, this is an excellent place to enjoy it before heading out.

Going Further: Consider extending your hike to Woodburn Falls and Lower Falls in the eastern part of Lacamas Park. Or head just west of Round Lake to Heritage Park to take on the 7-mile roundtrip, mixed-use Lacamas Heritage Trail. This flat gravel path hugs the shoreline of Lacamas Lake—an excellent option for cyclists.

MILES AND DIRECTIONS

0.0 From the north end of the parking lot, head north across the footbridge. Follow the trail along the road and fence line, turning right to follow the sidewalk up NE 35th Avenue.

0.2 Turn right onto the gravel trail.

0.5 Reach the lakeview dock. Stay on the wide, main path, ignoring side trails.

0.7 Turn left, then immediately take a second left for the Camas Lily Loop.

0.9 Stay right for the Camas Lily Loop at all trail junctions.

1.2 Turn right onto the forest road and continue straight along it, ignoring side trails.

1.6 Approach a potentially confusing intersection. Continue straight, following the sign for Round Lake Loop. Then turn immediately left and approach the fenceline for a view of Pothole Falls below.

1.7 At the fenceline, turn right (northwest) to follow the creek to Round Lake.

1.9 Reach a bench overlooking the lake. Cross the dam and continue north to the trailhead.

LOCAL INTEREST

Grains of Wrath Brewery: From light, refreshing lagers to hop-forward IPAs, this brewery crafts a range of award-winning styles well worth seeking out. Expect a full menu featuring bowls, burgers, sandwiches, and more. Address: 230 NE 5th Avenue, Camas, WA; Phone: (360) 210-5717; Web: www.gowbeer.com

Steigerwald Lake Wildlife Refuge: Seeking a more peaceful nature walk near Camas? Steigerwald is the answer. Located on the Columbia River, this refuge is excellent for spotting birds and other wildlife. Directions: From Camas, head east on WA-14 for 3

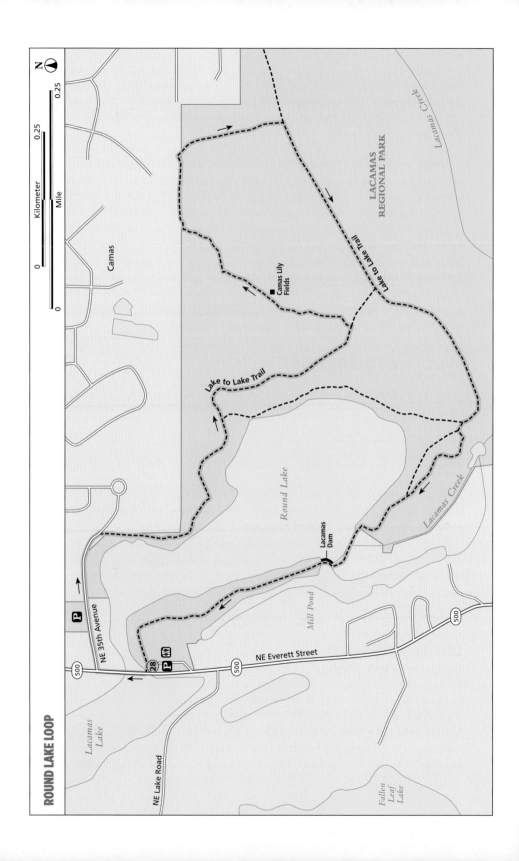

ROUND LAKE LOOP

N

Kilometer
0   0.25

Mile
0   0.25

Camas

LACAMAS
REGIONAL PARK

Lacamas Creek

Lacamas Creek

Lake to Lake Trail

Camas Lily
Fields

Lake to Lake Trail

Round Lake

Lacamas Lake

NE 35th Avenue

Lacamas Dam

Mill Pond

NE Everett Street

NE Lake Road

Fallen
Leaf
Lake

500

28

A small bridge over the wetlands is shaded by a green umbrella of leafy trees.

miles. Take a right into the entrance just after mile marker 18. Phone: (503) 231-6120; Web: www.fws.gov/refuge/Steigerwald_Lake

LODGING

Hilton Vancouver Washington: Full-service hotel with park-view suites in Downtown Vancouver. Located across the street from Esther Short Park and Loowit Brewing, this hotel's central location can't be beat. Address: 301 W 6th St, Vancouver, WA; Phone: (360) 993-4500; Web: www3.hilton.com

CENTRAL WASHINGTON

Just east of the Cascade Mountains, Central Washington is where urbanites head for relaxation and adventure. Cities like Wenatchee and Yakima have rich histories in agricultural production, an identity that continues on even today. Now, these cities have a new identity to bring in commerce: as a recreation destination. The growing prestige of the Columbia Valley wine scene has put cities like Chelan on the map for many wine connoisseurs. Embracing tourism has even saved towns like Leavenworth—Washington's Bavarian wonderland—from economic downturn. And with a rise in the ability to work remotely, many suburbanites are moving across the mountain pass to escape the city grind.

A terrain defined by shrub-steppe and rugged canyons is contrasted by lush irrigated farmlands. Snug to the foothills of the towering Cascade Mountains, Central Washington is also a winter playground for many, as lowland hiking trails transition to snowshoeing and cross-country skiing destinations. After delighting in the gastronomic pleasures of the region, a walk in the woods is always a welcome option!

Pass by the Cowiche Canyon organic hop farm and get a peek into a real working hop farm.

29 YAKIMA GREENWAY

Hike a section of the Yakima Greenway as it follows the snaking Yakima River. With parks on both ends, this route is perfect for families, offering educational opportunities and recreation activities.

Elevation gain: 50 feet
Distance: 2.5 miles
Hiking time: 1-2 hours
Difficulty: Easy
Seasons: Year round
Trail surface: Paved path, mowed grass
Land status: City park
Nearest town: Yakima
Other users: Cyclists, joggers
Water availability: Yes, at restrooms

Canine compatibility: Dogs must remain on leash along Yakima Greenway. Off-leash area available at Sherman Park.
Fees and permits: None
Map: Yakima Greenway Foundation: www.yakimagreenway.org/maps
Trail contact: Yakima Greenway Foundation: (509) 453-8280
Trailhead GPS: N46.6022 W120.4756

FINDING THE TRAILHEAD

From I-82, take exit 33B for Yakima Avenue toward Terrace Heights. Keep left at the fork to turn left onto E Yakima Avenue. Drive 0.1 miles, then turn right onto S 18th Street. Drive 0.1 miles, then turn left into Sarg Hubbard Park. Begin your hike from the restrooms.

WHAT TO SEE

The Yakima Greenway Trail spans 10 miles of paved trail, following sections of the Yakima and Naches Rivers through the heart of Yakima. From its hub at Sarg Hubbard Park, the trail stretches north towards Selah, and south into Union Gap. Traveling south on the trail, you can make a lollipop loop through the ever-green and peaceful Yakima Arboretum.

Sarg Hubbard Park makes for an ideal starting point with picnic facilities, restrooms, water, and even a stocked fishing pond! Head south through the park over the bridge towards a viewing platform. A quick climb up the wooden structure offers overhead views of Rotary Lake and the city of Yakima in the distance. Further down the trail you might notice pieces of the Gamefield Jogging Course, which pop up throughout Sarg Hubbard Park. Each station offers a different exercise, together creating a parcourse. Feel free to add the extra challenge to your walk!

At 0.2 miles, meet up with the Yakima Greenway and get your first glimpse of the Yakima River. The elevated paved trail follows the curve of the river to the east, with marshlands to the west along the edge of Buchanan Lake. The marsh is home to a variety of birds, and likely your walk will have a red-winged blackbird soundtrack. Across the river on the east bank is Yakima Sportsman State Park—another excellent birding destination.

Once you come to a junction in the trail at 0.9 miles, continue on the paved path to the right, leading into the arboretum. The Yakima Area Arboretum's mission statement calls the 46-acre park a, "living museum of over 1,000 specimens," with multiple display gardens dotting the property. A literal oasis in the often scorching Yakima Valley, enter the

Trees at the Arboretum offer plenty of cooling shade.

Rotary Lake in Sarg Hubbard Park is a popular fishing spot.

arboretum under the cool green shade of towering trees. Once you hit the green lawn, the paved path continues left to Sherman Park—an off-leash dog area, and the Yakima Humane Society. Instead, at the junction, turn right onto the mowed grass pathway into the arboretum.

There isn't a "correct" way to explore the arboretum, but we will describe a loop that goes through the heart of the arboretum. Follow along, or pick up a garden map at the visitor center and choose your own adventure. At 1.1 miles, you'll come to the Joyful Garden, an example of the formal Japanese garden that includes a water feature, pavilion, and traditional plants. After passing through the garden, you'll continue on along the mowed path through the arboretum's multiple tree collections. Stay on the lookout for highlights including ginkgos and the living fossil: the dawn redwood. In the fall, be sure to search out the golden fronds of western larches. Continue on the main path as it curves through the arboretum. You'll soon meet up with the main paved trail. Turn left and continue back to Sarg Hubbard Park.

MILES AND DIRECTIONS

0.0   From the restrooms at Sarg Hubbard Park, head south on the paved path. Take the first left to walk over the bridge overlooking Rotary Lake.

0.1   After crossing the bridge turn left, then immediately right to continue walking south.

0.2   Turn right onto the Yakima Greenway and head south.

0.9   Turn right at a junction to follow the paved path into Yakima Area Arboretum.

1.0   Enter the arboretum, and follow the mowed grass paths in a clockwise loop.

1.5   Return to the previous junction and retrace your steps to the trailhead.

LOCAL INTEREST

Yakima Humane Society: Feeling lonesome on your hike? Consider stopping in to Yakima Humane Society to take advantage of the public dog-walking program.

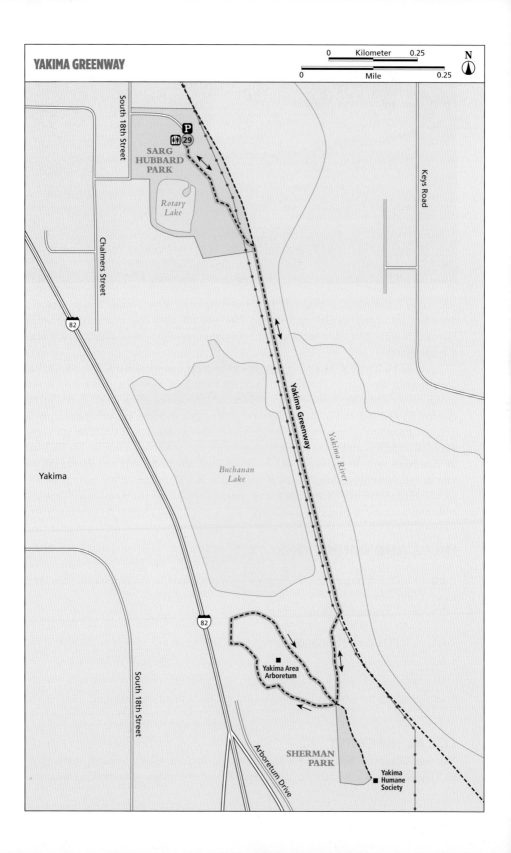

0 Kilometer 0.25

0 Mile 0.25

N

South 18th Street

SARG
HUBBARD
PARK

P
29

Rotary
Lake

Chalmers Street

82

Keys Road

Yakima Greenway

Yakima River

Yakima

Buchanan
Lake

82

South 18th Street

Yakima Area
Arboretum

Arboretum Drive

SHERMAN
PARK

Yakima Humane
Society

The Yakima River rushes past the Yakima Greenway trail.

Volunteers 18 or older with a valid driver's license can take a friendly pooch for a walk along the Greenway. You might leave Yakima with a new best friend! Address: 2405 West Birchfield Rd., Yakima, WA; Phone: (509) 457-6854; Web: www.yakimahumane.org

Los Hernández Tamales: A James Beard Award winner, Los Hernández has been serving authentic tamales since 1990. Consider grabbing a package of frozen tamales to take home! Address: 3706 Main St., Union Gap, WA; Phone: (509)457-6003, Web: www .loshernandeztamales.com

LODGING

Oxford Suites Yakima: Located on the Yakima Greenway and close to Sarg Hubbard Park. Offering 108 spacious guest suites including rooms ideal for extended stays. Address: 1701 E Yakima Ave., Yakima, WA; Phone:(509) 457- 9000; Web: www.oxford suitesyakima.com

30 COWICHE CANYON TRAIL

Cross nine bridges over Cowiche Creek as you walk through a 3-mile shrub-steppe canyon near Yakima. Spring wildflowers and brilliant fall colors make for an excellent shoulder-season hike.

Elevation gain: 500 feet (including Winery Trail); 100 feet (Cowiche Canyon only)
Distance: 7 miles out-and-back (including Winery Trail); 5.4 miles out-and-back (Cowiche Canyon only)
Hiking time: 3–4 hours
Difficulty: Moderate due to elevation gain on Winery Trail; easy if hiking Cowiche Canyon only
Seasons: Year round (may encounter ice and snow during winter)
Trail surface: Gravel path

Land status: Cowiche Canyon Conservancy; Bureau of Land Management
Nearest town: Yakima
Other users: Equestrians, cyclists, joggers
Water availability: None
Canine compatibility: Dogs must remain on leash
Fees and permits: None
Map: Cowiche Canyon Conservancy - Cowiche Canyon/Uplands Map: www.cowichecanyon.org/trails/
Trail contact: Cowiche Canyon Conservancy: (509) 248-5065
Trailhead GPS: N46.6222 W120.6148

FINDING THE TRAILHEAD

From I-82, take exit 31A for US 12 West. Keep right to continue on exit 31A and merge onto US 12 West. Drive 3.6 miles, then turn left onto Ackley Road, followed immediately by a left turn onto W Powerhouse Road. Drive 0.2 miles, then turn right onto Cowiche Canyon Road. Drive 2.2 miles and park in the gravel lot on the right (the last mile is on a gravel road). The trail begins from the west side of the East Trailhead parking lot.

If you'd prefer to avoid driving the gravel road, park at the West Trailhead off of Weikel Road.

WHAT TO SEE

Featuring towering andesite and basalt walls, Cowiche Canyon (it's pronounced Cow-itchy) is an unmissable urban hike within 20 minutes' drive of downtown Yakima. Families, runners, mountain bikers, pedestrians, and equestrians alike will get a kick out of this rocky canyon ramble.

From the East Trailhead, follow the trail west into Cowiche Canyon where you'll immediately pass by the Cowiche Canyon Organic Hop Farm. Welcome to hop country! If you've ever wondered why IPAs are so popular in Washington, it's because 75 percent of the nation's hops are grown in the Yakima Valley. Visit during late summer to witness the hop harvest. Better yet, come during fall for the annual Fresh Hop Ale Festival, when Yakima celebrates the local hop harvest by inviting dozens of brewers to create beers made with fresh-from-the-bine hops. These special brews showcase the very best of the Northwest in liquid form.

Another reason to visit Cowiche Canyon during fall: the colors. Mountain ash and aspen trees turn brilliant shades of crimson and gold every October. Spring and early summer are delightful as well, when yellow balsamroot and indigo lupine bloom along

A group of equestrians rides through the canyon as seen from the Winery Trail spur.

the slopes. Like all of Central and Eastern Washington, Yakima experiences "real" seasons—hot summers and cold, snowy winters. Mid-summer is best avoided due to high temps that can reach 100 degrees (and a higher chance of rattlesnake encounters). Bring plenty of water and sunscreen if hiking during the warmer months. During winter, plan on walking through snow and ice.

The trail follows an old railroad bed—once used to transport fruit—along Cowiche Creek. After 1 mile you'll reach a junction with the signed Winery Trail on the right. Gaining 400 feet over 0.8 miles, this optional trail is an excellent way to elevate your workout with the reward of wine tasting (see info on Wilridge Winery below). Not only home to hop country, Yakima has long been known as Washington wine country as well. Over half of Washington State's wine grapes are grown in the Yakima Valley. At Wilridge Winery, you can walk through a working vineyard to sample from the onsite wine bar and tasting room.

Continue walking west on the Cowiche Canyon Trail. As you wander farther into the wild western reaches of Cowiche Canyon, its walls rise up on either side of the trail. Away from city sounds, you're surrounded by the canyon's shrub-steppe landscape in the rainshadow of the Cascade Mountains. Distinct from deserts (where vegetation is sparse), shrub-steppe areas like Cowiche Canyon receive enough precipitation to sustain diverse vegetation, from sagebrush and wildflowers to oak and aspen. In Cowiche Canyon, these unique grasslands are protected by a nonprofit land trust. The Cowiche Canyon Conservancy (CCC) protects over 5,000 acres of shrub-steppe habitat in the Yakima area.

Once you've walked the length of the canyon, turn around and retrace your steps. Perhaps one of the CCC's over 30 miles of trails will entice you to extend your hike along the canyon rim. Each of these trails offers excellent views down the canyon, but only one

COWICHE CANYON TRAIL

N

1 Kilometer 1

1 Mile 0

0

Zimmerman Road

Yakima

Dahl Road

Schuler Grade Road

Naches Heights Road

Ehler Road

North Weikel Road

Summitview Road

Cowiche Canyon Trail

Cowiche Creek

Tasting Room

Winery Trail

Cowiche Canyon Trail

30

Cowiche Canyon Hop Farm

Cowiche Canyon Road

The trail crosses the snaking Cowiche Creek over a series of bridges.

of them offers wine. If you missed it on the way out, the Winery Trail will still be waiting on your way back to the trailhead.

MILES AND DIRECTIONS

- **0.0** Begin by walking west on the Cowiche Canyon Trail.
- **1.0** Turn right onto the Winery Trail.
- **1.5** Enter the vineyard and turn left to follow the road north. Then turn right to walk east to the tasting room.
- **1.8** Reach the winery tasting room. Retrace your steps to the main Cowiche Canyon Trail.
- **2.6** Turn right and continue west on the Cowiche Canyon Trail.
- **4.3** Reach the end of the Cowiche Canyon Trail and return to the trailhead.

LOCAL INTEREST

Wilridge Winery: Walk to a plateau-top winery 400 feet above the Cowiche Canyon Trail for a taste of the local terroir. Not up for the climb? You can drive instead. Address: 250 Ehler Rd., Yakima, WA; Phone: (509) 966-0686; Web: www.wilridgewinery.com

Cowiche Creek Brewing: This family friendly beer farm grows its own hops and barley, serving hop-centric brews from a hilltop taproom. Address: 514 Thompson Rd., Cowiche, WA; Phone: (509) 678-0324; Web: www.cowichecreekbrewing.com

LODGING

Wilridge Vineyard Farmhouse Guest Rooms: Stay at the winery via Airbnb! Rooms are available in the 100-year-old farmhouse. Address: 250 Ehler Rd., Yakima, WA; Phone: (509) 966-0686; Web: www.wilridgewinery.com

31 BLACKBIRD ISLAND

Stroll among cottonwood trees and watch for wildlife at Blackbird Island, a riverside escape just steps from downtown Leavenworth.

Elevation gain: 75 feet
Distance: 2-mile double lollipop
Hiking time: 1 hour
Difficulty: Easy
Seasons: Year round
Trail surface: Dirt path, paved path
Land status: City park
Nearest town: Leavenworth
Other users: Cyclists
Water availability: Yes, at restrooms

Canine compatibility: Dogs must remain on leash
Fees and permits: None
Map: Map to Leavenworth Area Parks, Trails, and Beaches - City of Leavenworth
Trail contact: City of Leavenworth Parks: (509) 548-5275
Trailhead GPS: N47°35.647' W120°39.487'

FINDING THE TRAILHEAD

From US 2, head south on 9th Street through downtown Leavenworth. After traveling 0.1 mile from the highway, turn left on Main Street. Continue 0.1 mile to the parking lot at the end of the road.

WHAT TO SEE

Few towns in the state are more lively than Leavenworth. A festive feeling—fueled by the constant rotation of Bavarian-themed events and European alpine architecture—greets visitors upon arrival. It seems there's always something worth celebrating here, and why not? Located alongside the winding Wenatchee River in the shadow of the Cascade Mountains, Leavenworth is a picture-perfect vacation destination for all seasons. Skiers, hikers, kayakers, and retail therapy enthusiasts alike can all find something to love in Leavenworth.

Whether you're visiting for an afternoon or the week, the best way to navigate town (and enjoy the nature nearby) is on foot. Fortunately, a string of parks seamlessly connect downtown Leavenworth to its riverfront for access to year-round urban hiking. Take a leisurely summer stroll or snowy wintertime walk. Regardless of the season, you can enjoy these forest paths for an hour or more before returning to Leavenworth for refreshments.

Beginning from Waterfront Park, a wide dirt path sets off through the trees. Enjoy peek-a-boo Wenatchee River views as you head south, then west, passing a playground and seasonal restrooms (open spring through fall). The path widens into a bench-lined promenade before coming to the battlement, an overlook above the river. Pause here for mountain and river views, and to fill up water bottles at the fountain. Then continue across the bridge to Blackbird Island.

An interpretive sign at the entrance to Blackbird Island explains its creation. The island emerged from silt accumulations when a mill pond was drained in the 1930s, sprouting life in the form of grasses, shrubs, and small cottonwoods. Today, nature has fully reclaimed the site. Black cottonwood trees now dominate the island alongside large conifers like ponderosa pine. Hang a left at the sign to follow the Wenatchee River. Visible in the distance, Wedge Mountain and its Cascade cousins tower over The Enchantments—a

Hike along the Wenatchee
River on Blackbird Island.

The banks of the Wenatchee River with Wedge Mountain behind.

legendary alpine lakes basin outside Leavenworth (and home to the most sought-after backpacking permits in the state). Consider that an adventure for another day.

Cross a second bridge to enter Enchantment Park. Less notorious than its namesake lakes, this city park is nonetheless full of little surprises. Stick to the river as you continue south along the Bear Trail. Bears are occasionally spotted near the river here, so keep an eye out! Of course, you're more likely to encounter the various birds, beavers, and fish that call this slice of the Wenatchee River home. Pass a few pocket beaches along the way while listening to the call of chickadees in the trees.

The trail turns to pavement as it veers north, entering a sports complex. Sloping hillsides here are a favorite spot for wintertime sledding. Ball fields, a playground, a bike pump track, and restrooms round out the park's many amenities, making Enchantment Park a great place for rest and recreation. The park also provides alternative trailhead parking for access to Blackbird Island.

Return via the northern Enchantment Trail to make a loop. Then cross the bridge back to Blackbird Island, taking the Channel Trail left to make two loops in one walk. Before you know it you'll be back at Waterfront Park on the edge of downtown Leavenworth. From here the town is yours: grab lunch at any one of the German restaurants in town, or lift a liter stein at one of Leavenworth's many pubs (see Local Interest for our suggestion). Prost!

MILES AND DIRECTIONS

0.0 From the south end of the parking lot, head south (right) on the trail.

0.2 Reach the battlement overlook. Turn left and cross the bridge to Blackbird Island.

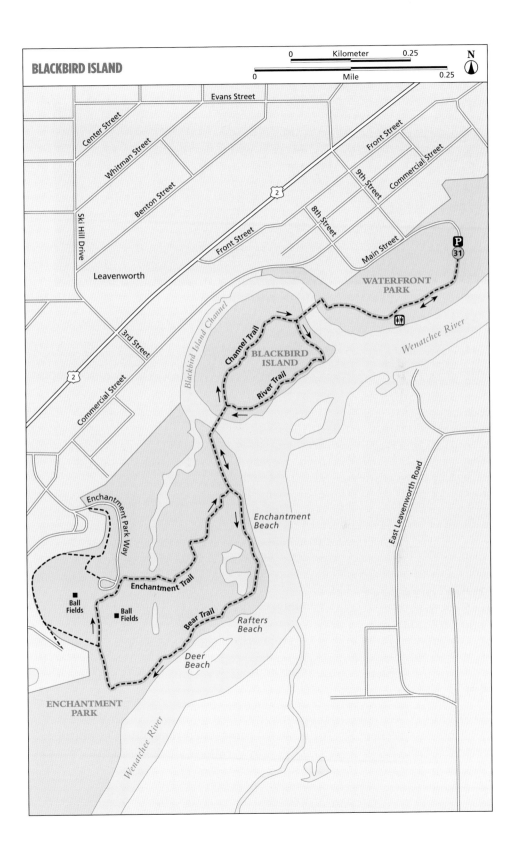

BLACKBIRD ISLAND

0   Kilometer   0.25
0   Mile   0.25
N

Evans Street

Center Street
Whitman Street
Benton Street

Front Street
9th Street
Commercial Street
8th Street
Main Street

2

Ski Hill Drive

Leavenworth

Front Street

P
31

WATERFRONT
PARK

3rd Street

2

Commercial Street

Blackbird Island Channel

Channel Trail

BLACKBIRD
ISLAND

River Trail

Wenatchee River

Enchantment Park Way

Enchantment Beach

East Leavenworth Road

Enchantment Trail

Ball
Fields

Ball
Fields

Bear Trail

Rafters
Beach

Deer
Beach

ENCHANTMENT
PARK

Wenatchee River

Downtown Leavenworth as seen from a bridge over the channel.

0.3 Turn left (south) at the junction, then immediately stay left at a second junction to complete the loop in a clockwise direction.

0.5 Stay left at the junction with Hot Sands Trail. Then turn left at a second junction and cross the bridge to Enchantment Park.

0.6 Turn left onto the Bear Trail.

0.9 Reach Rafters Beach. Continue left on the Bear Trail along the water.

1.0 Dirt path turns to pavement.

1.1 Continue straight, passing between the softball fields to reach the restrooms at Enchantment Park.

1.2 Walk around the eastern edge of the parking lot, then head east on the Enchantment Trail. Stay left at the intersection with the Rafters Trail.

1.5 Complete the Enchantment Trail loop. Return across the bridge to Blackbird Island.

1.6 Take the Channel Trail left to complete the Blackbird Island loop.

1.8 Finish the Blackbird Island loop and cross the bridge to Waterfront Park. Return the way you came.

LOCAL INTEREST

Munchen Haus: Our favorite Bavarian-themed beer garden and brat spot in Leavenworth, Munchen Haus serves local Icicle Brewing pints alongside German sausages and pretzels in a heated outdoor beer garden. Address: 709 Front St., Leavenworth, WA; Phone: (509) 548-1158; Web: www.munchenhaus.com

LODGING

Leavenworth Village Inn: This modern, downtown Leavenworth hotel is located within walking distance of the trail, shops, and restaurants. Address: 1016 Commercial St., Leavenworth, WA; Phone: (509) 548-6620; Web: www.leavenworthvillageinn.com

32 APPLE CAPITAL LOOP TRAIL

Explore Wenatchee's waterfront on the banks of the Columbia River to discover city parks, a sculpture garden, and the plentiful offerings of Pybus Public Market.

Elevation gain: Minimal
Distance: 3.8 miles out-and-back (or up to 10-mile loop)
Hiking time: 2 hours
Difficulty: Easy
Seasons: Year round
Trail surface: Paved path
Land status: Chelan County PUD Parks Department; city park
Nearest town: Wenatchee
Other users: Joggers, cyclists

Water availability: Yes, at restrooms
Canine compatibility: Dogs must remain on leash
Fees and permits: None
Map: Apple Capital Loop Trail - Chelan County PUD
Trail contact: Chelan County PUD: (509) 661-4551
Trailhead GPS: N47°26.731' W120°19.087'

FINDING THE TRAILHEAD

From US 2, take WA-285 S/N Wenatchee Avenue for Wenatchee. Drive 1.3 miles, then turn left onto Hawley Street. Drive 0.5 miles, then turn left onto Walla Walla Avenue. Continue 0.3 miles, then turn left into Walla Walla Point Park. At an immediate intersection turn left, passing the tennis courts. Follow the parkway 0.2 miles to the trailhead parking lot. The trailhead is at the northeast corner of the lot.

WHAT TO SEE

The Wenatchee Valley has long been known as the "Apple Capital of the World" with orchards covering the surrounding hillsides. In celebration of the city's moniker, a trail along the riverfront on both sides of the Columbia now bears its name. Wenatchee's Apple Capital Loop Trail covers 10 miles of paved trail along the banks of the Columbia River. The western side of the loop makes an excellent morning or afternoon stroll, through the lush string of city parks to Pybus Public Market. The route we describe has access to playgrounds, multiple green spaces, benches, and even ice cream, making it ideal for families.

Begin at Walla Walla Point Park. This large, well-maintained waterfront park has everything from a swimming beach to ball fields making it a favorite for residents. Start your urban hike by trekking out onto the point that gives this park its name. A silt build-up from the nearby confluence of the Wenatchee River into the Columbia, Walla Walla Point is now home to a number of birds and plants including cottonwood trees. Explore the point, then return to meet back up with the Apple Capital Loop Trail.

The wide paved path is in high use by joggers, cyclists, pet owners, and families. There is very little shade on the trail, offering expansive views of the Columbia River and surrounding foothills, but it could be a scorcher during hot summer days. Plan accordingly and consider either a morning or sunset walk.

The trail passes the Columbia River through Walla Walla Point Park.

When you reach the end of Walla Walla Point Park, you will transition immediately into Linden Tree Park. A quiet stream creates a wetland haven, and also an ideal area to launch kayaks and canoes from. Wenatchee Row and Paddle Club operates their boathouses from this area. "The Barn," an old log structure, is particularly picturesque from the wooden bridge that crosses the small stream.

From here, the Apple Capital Loop Trail continues onto a greenway promenade past restaurants, hotels, and apartments. Though not a park, this stretch is not lacking for natural beauty as the grassy areas and flower beds continue to surround the trail. After passing the tree-lined US Bank Plaza, you'll come to the northern end of Wenatchee Riverfront Park.

You might notice some train tracks running through the park. This is the Wenatchee Riverfront Railway, a seasonally operated rideable miniature railway. Donated by Nile Saunders in 1988, the train originally ran through his pear orchard. Check the schedule ahead of time to see if the train will be running during your visit. Wenatchee Riverfront Park is also home to an outdoor sculpture garden—brochures are available in the park to learn about the pieces.

Once you come to the boat launch at the end of the park, take the crosswalk on your right and head towards the large building ahead. This is Pybus Public Market. If you've worked up an appetite, this is a great place to grab lunch, or give into your sweet tooth with some gelato. With live music every Friday, and a calendar packed with events, Pybus Market is always buzzing with things to do. A great place to take a breather, the market also makes for an ideal turn around point. Return the way you came back to Walla Walla Point Park.

Going Further: There's still plenty to explore on the Apple Capital Loop Trail. Bike rentals are available at Pybus Market, making the full 10-mile loop more manageable. Alternately, consider parking at the Wenatchee Confluence State Park, north of Walla Walla Point Park, to add on some mileage.

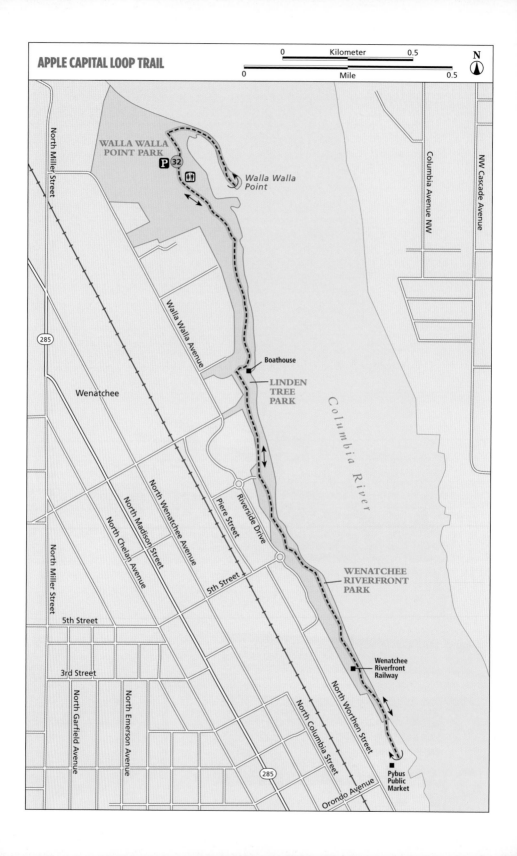

Kilometer

0   0.5

0   0.5
Mile

N

WALLA WALLA
POINT PARK

P 32

Walla Walla
Point

North Miller Street

Columbia Avenue NW

NW Cascade Avenue

285

Wenatchee

Walla Walla Avenue

Boathouse

LINDEN
TREE
PARK

Columbia River

North Wenatchee Avenue

North Madison Street

North Chelan Avenue

Piere Street

Riverside Drive

5th Street

WENATCHEE
RIVERFRONT
PARK

North Miller Street

5th Street

3rd Street

North Garfield Avenue

North Emerson Avenue

285

North Columbia Street

North Worthen Street

Orondo Avenue

Wenatchee
Riverfront
Railway

Pybus
Public
Market

An outdoor sculpture collection lines part of the trail near the public market.

MILES AND DIRECTIONS

0.0 From the trailhead at Walla Walla Point Park, head north on the Apple Capital Loop Trail.

0.1 Turn right at a junction to walk out on the point.

0.3 At the end of the point, turn around and retrace your steps to the trailhead. Then continue south on the loop trail.

2.2 Reach the restrooms across the street from Pybus Public Market. Turn around here and retrace your steps to the trailhead.

LOCAL INTEREST

Pybus Public Market: This farmers market is home to multiple restaurants including the popular taphouse for Wenatchee Valley Brewing. Local artisans, produce, and entertainment all come together in a unique community space. Address: 3 N Worthen St., Wenatchee, WA; Phone: (509) 888-3900; Web: pybuspublicmarket.org

LODGING

SpringHill Suites by Marriott Wenatchee: Located 1 mile from Walla Walla Point Park and Apple Capital Loop Trail. On a main thoroughfare near eateries and services. Address: 1730 N Wenatchee Ave., Wenatchee, WA; Phone: (509) 667-2775; Web: www .marriott.com/wenatchee

33 SADDLE ROCK TRAIL

Enjoy bird's-eye Columbia River and Valley views from nearly 2,000 feet above Wenatchee on this short, steep urban hike to an iconic saddle between two peaks.

Elevation gain: 890 feet
Distance: 3.2 miles out-and-back
Hiking time: 2 hours
Difficulty: Difficult due to steep elevation gain
Seasons: Year round (traction may be necessary during winter)
Trail surface: Gravel, hard-packed dirt path
Land status: City park
Nearest town: Wenatchee
Other users: Mountain bikers, equestrians, joggers
Water availability: Yes, at restrooms

Canine compatibility: Dogs must remain on leash
Fees and permits: None
Map: Wenatchee Foothills Trails - Chelan-Douglas Land Trust
Trail contact: City of Wenatchee Parks: (509) 888-3284; Chelan-Douglas Land Trust: www.cdland trust.org/trails-access/trails/wenatchee-foothills-trails/saddle -rock-trails
Trailhead GPS: N47°23.787' W120°19.844'

FINDING THE TRAILHEAD

From Pybus Public Market in downtown Wenatchee, head south on Orondo Avenue for 0.8 mile. Turn left on Miller Street, then drive 1.2 miles. Turn right onto Circle Road and continue 0.2 mile to the trailhead parking lot.

WHAT TO SEE

Visible from downtown Wenatchee, Saddle Rock is a prominent local landmark rising high into the southwestern skyline. Get your heart rate up on the short yet rewarding climb to the top. Impressive from afar, it's an exhilarating experience to stand atop the saddle with sweeping views across the shrub-steppe landscape.

Saddle Rock is perhaps best hiked during spring due to its bright balsamroot blooms. The mild, pleasant shoulder-season weather is a bonus as well. Regardless of seasonality, Saddle Rock makes for an excellent urban hiking destination year round. Begin near sunrise or sunset during summer for a cooler, less crowded hike. And if hiking during winter, traction footwear or snowshoes may be necessary. Check current conditions at the Chelan-Douglas Land Trust (see Trail contact) website.

Set out from the large parking area at Saddle Rock Gateway. Constructed in 2017, this previously undeveloped trailhead now offers ample parking, restrooms, water, and a picnic shelter as a City of Wenatchee park. You're likely to find trail users of all kinds here, from families with young children to endurance runners and after-work walkers. Due to its proximity to the city and easy access, Saddle Rock Trail has an urban vibe from the get-go. But don't let that fool you—this is a serious little trek into the wild Wenatchee foothills.

Your destination—the andesite summit of Saddle Rock—is visible from the trailhead. Follow the wide gravel path north, pausing to admire the donor monument at 0.1 mile. Thanks to overwhelming community support, the land Saddle Rock rests on was

acquired by the Chelan-Douglas Land Trust and City of Wenatchee in 2011, protecting it for future generations.

There are many ways to reach Saddle Rock. Because unofficial "social" trails contribute to erosion and damage the fragile environment, users should stick to the main trail at all times. However, there are places along this trail where it's unclear which trail to take. We've noted significant intersections in the Miles and Directions section. When in doubt, stick to the widest, most well-traveled path.

Gravel eventually gives way to hard-packed, sun-dried earth. After a fairly gentle first 0.5 mile, the trail rounds a bend and steepens significantly. Along the way you'll be accompanied by sage brush, lupin, and balsamroot. At 1 mile come to a junction. The steep, narrow trail to the right is a shortcut to the saddle, gaining over 100 feet in a short distance. You can make a loop via this trail, but we suggest sticking to the wider, gentler path left to lengthen your hike (and take it easier on the knees).

Climb the series of rolling switchbacks to gain the ridge at 1.4 miles. Hang a right here, walking along the ridgeline to an open viewpoint at 1.5 miles. Beyond, the volcanic stone sentinels loom. Wenatchi-P'squosa legend says that Coyote turned Black Bear and Grizzly Bear to stone after tiring of their arguing. Ravens soar high above. Below, the city of Wenatchee blankets the valley, bisected by the deep blue of the Columbia River. This spot makes for a great turn around point, especially if hiking with children or dogs.

The trail narrows from here as it approaches Saddle Rock. If proceeding past this overlook, you'll pass a few trees and soon come to an unmarked junction. Take the lower trail to the right, descending slightly to the saddle. Watch your footing along this sheer section. Upon reaching the saddle, enjoy stunning valley views before returning the way you came.

SADDLE ROCK TRAIL

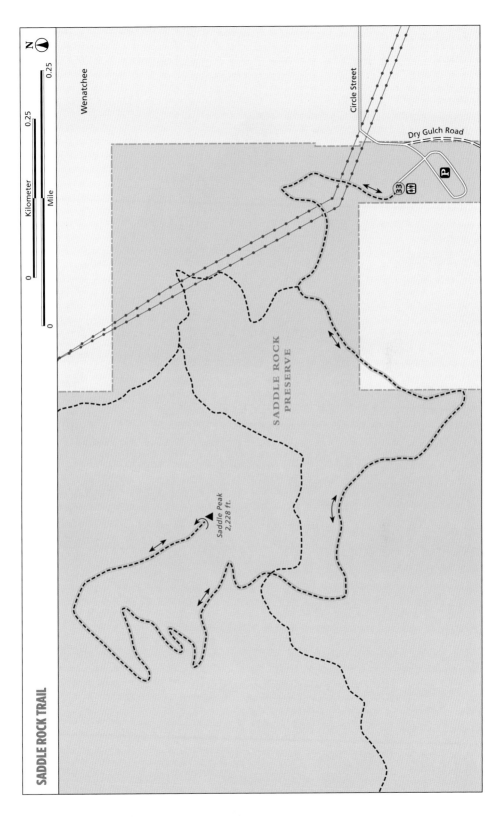

Wenatchee

Circle Street

Dry Gulch Road

SADDLE ROCK
PRESERVE

Saddle Peak
2,228 ft.

33

P

N

Kilometer
0   0.25   0.25

Mile
0   0.25

The hillsides of the Saddle Rock Trail come into full bloom in mid-spring.

MILES AND DIRECTIONS

0.0 Hike north from the signed trailhead.

0.1 Stay left at the junction.

0.3 Turn left at the junction.

0.9 Stay left on the wide main path.

1.4 Turn right at the junction

1.5 Come to an open viewpoint. Turn around here, or continue carefully to the saddle via the lower trail to the right.

1.6 Reach Saddle Rock. Return the way you came.

LOCAL INTEREST

Sage Hills Hike: For a longer excursion through rolling hills alive with spring wildflowers, Sage Hills can't be beat. Address: 525-521 Sage Hills Dr., Wenatchee, WA; Phone: (509) 667-9708; Web: www.cdlandtrust.org/trails-access/trails/wenatchee-foothills-trails/sage-hill-trails

McGlinn's Public House: Decked out with eclectic local memorabilia, McGlinn's serves wood-fired pizza, pub grub, and local brews in a lively atmosphere. Address: 111 Orondo Ave., Wenatchee, WA; Phone: (509) 663-9073; Web: www.mcglinns.com

LODGING

Coast Wenatchee Center Hotel: Conveniently located in the center of downtown Wenatchee within walking distance of restaurants, breweries, and the waterfront. Less than 3 miles from the Saddle Rock trailhead. Address: 201 N Wenatchee Ave., Wenatchee, WA; Phone: (509) 662-1234; Web: www.coasthotels.com

34 CHELAN RIVER GORGE

Stretch your legs on a hike through shrub-steppe ecosystem along the Chelan River with views of the Lake Chelan Dam and Chelan Butte.

Elevation gain: 160 feet
Distance: 3.1 miles out-and-back
Hiking time: 2 hours
Difficulty: Easy
Seasons: Year round
Trail surface: Gravel, paved path
Land status: Chelan County PUD Parks Department
Nearest town: Chelan
Other users: Joggers

Water availability: Not available
Canine compatibility: Dogs must remain on leash
Fees and permits: None
Map: Chelan Riverwalk Loop and Reach 1 Trail - Chelan County PUD
Trail contact: Chelan County PUD: (509) 682-2581
Trailhead GPS: N47°50.016′ W120°00.840′

FINDING THE TRAILHEAD

From E Woodin Avenue (WA 150) in downtown Chelan, take Sanders Street south 0.2 miles. Cross the bridge, then immediately turn left onto S Farnham Street. Drive 0.2 mile, then turn left onto E Raymond Street. Park in the small gravel lot, about 200 feet ahead on the left.

WHAT TO SEE

Proving that there's more to do in the vacation town of Chelan than wine tasting and watersports, the Reach 1 Trail in the Chelan River Gorge is an excellent place to stretch your legs or go for a run. Incorporating educational information about the region's hydroelectric dams, geological history, and native cultures, this 3-mile trail will introduce visitors to another side of Chelan.

Start out on a paved path to the Dam Overlooks. From these viewpoints, you'll be able to take in the massive hydroelectric project, while staring down the depth of Lake Chelan. In the Salish language, Chelan translates to "deep water," and the lake lives up to the name: Chelan is the nation's third-deepest lake. Continue along the trail as you follow the lake's primary outflow, the Chelan River.

At 0.4 miles you'll come to a large gravel parking lot. This is an alternate access point, and also serves as parking for the Chelan Butte Trail system. The emerald slopes of the butte rise above you, and it's worth pausing to see if you can spot paragliders taking off from this popular launch spot. The parking lot also abuts a junkyard, which can be a bit of an eyesore. But there are plenty of other scenic sites to focus on instead. From here, the trail turns to gravel as it begins the descent to the riverbanks below.

This trail makes for a great shoulder-season hike—for multiple reasons. Fall colors set the gorge alight with hues of orange and gold, while in the spring the hillsides are dotted with lupine, mountain phlox, and balsamroot. There is also little to no tree cover on the trail, meaning summer heat will require extra sun protection and water. This area is also home to rattlesnakes that will often sun themselves on the open stretches of trail. For your safety, stay alert, keep all pets under control and on a leash, and make sure to keep children on the trail. If you do encounter a snake, give it a wide berth in which it can

Chelan River Gorge Trail takes you from the bluff to the river bed below.

Above the gorge looms the green rolling heights of Chelan Butte.

escape to safety. While it's often hard to remember, snakes are also scared of you. Please respect the wildlife and stay on designated trails.

Once you've hiked for 0.8 mile, the whole of the gorge will come into view. You'll be able to see the trail as it follows the curves of the slate blue Chelan River below. This next part of the trail is the steepest—something you'll be reminded of during the climb back out of the gorge on the way home. The trail cuts through the middle of the shrub-steppe environment. In the spring, pale yellow flowers bloom on the abundant bitterbrush, while a breeze might set the bunchgrass dancing. Watch for swallows as they dive and swoop along the river's edge, and listen closely for the curious call of the timid quail.

At 1 mile, you'll come to the first of three viewpoints along the river. Each offer benches, great for catching your breath or taking in the beauty of the rushing river. These are also locations of interpretive signs that are worth the read. From here, the rest of the trail follows the river to its terminus at a final overlook. Here, take in a small grove of trees, offering a bit of shade, before heading back the way you came.

Going Further: To extend your walk, head west from the trailhead to Sanders Street, then follow the sidewalk north 0.1 miles. Turn right on S Emerson Street to reach the Riverwalk Park Boat Launch. This area provides alternative parking and restrooms for the Chelan River Gorge Trail, and it connects to the 1-mile Riverwalk Park Loop Trail. The loop trail spans two bridges, entering Historic Downtown Chelan.

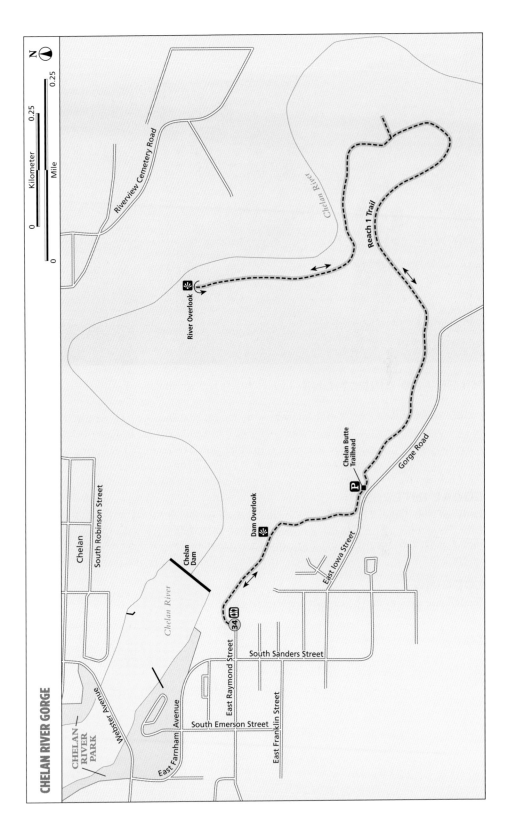

CHELAN RIVER GORGE

CHELAN RIVER PARK

Chelan

South Robinson Street

Chelan River

Chelan Dam

Webster Avenue

East Farnham Avenue

South Emerson Street

East Raymond Street

South Sanders Street

East Franklin Street

East Iowa Street

Dam Overlook

34

Chelan Butte Trailhead

P

Gorge Road

Reach 1 Trail

River Overlook

Chelan River

Riverview Cemetery Road

N

Kilometer
0   0.25

Mile
0   0.25

The Chelan River as seen from the trail in Spring.

MILES AND DIRECTIONS

0.0 Head northeast from the signed trailhead on the paved Chelan River Gorge Trail.

0.3 Reach the alternate trailhead parking lot. Continue east on the gravel trail.

1.6 Reach the end of the trail. Return the way you came.

LOCAL INTEREST

Lady of the Lake: Offering access to the remote village of Stehekin, Lady of the Lake cruises offer a boat ride like no other. Address: 1418 W Woodin Ave., Chelan, WA; Phone: (888) 682-4584; Web: www.ladyofthelake.com

LODGING

For lodging options in Chelan, visit www.lakechelan.com/stay.

EASTERN WASHINGTON

Though it's a significant portion of Washington State's overall landmass, Eastern Washington is sparsely populated. This arid landscape is primarily agricultural, with residents spread out across the area rather than living in densely populated cities (with a couple of notable exceptions). The city of Spokane is the state's second-largest city; the only other urban area of considerable size is the Tri-Cities. When urban areas are so spread out, a wide variety of wildlands is that much more accessible. Spokane and the Tri-Cities are both areas driven by rivers. The mighty Columbia River runs between the cities of Kennewick, Richland, and Pasco, before swinging west as it heads for the Pacific Ocean. Spokane has grown up from the banks of the Spokane River, a river that has eroded the earth into awe-inspiring canyons.

While cedars and Douglas fir dominate the damp forests of Western Washington, Eastern Washington's Inland Empire forests are filled with aromatic pines like the puzzle-piece-barked ponderosa. Sagebrush covers the rugged hillsides of ancient glacial-flood carved basalt in the Columbia Plateau. Here, the west is truly wild, and just beyond the doorstep of urban living.

Balsamroot bloom among the grasses during spring on Badger Mountain.

35 RICHLAND RIVERFRONT TRAIL

Take a walk in Washington wine country on this flat, blacktop trail beside the Columbia River—a family favorite in the Tri-Cities.

Elevation gain: Minimal
Distance: 3.6 miles out-and-back
Hiking time: 2 hours
Difficulty: Easy
Seasons: Year round
Trail surface: Paved path
Land status: City park
Nearest town: Richland
Other users: Cyclists, joggers

Water availability: Yes, at restrooms
Canine compatibility: Dogs must remain on leash
Fees and permits: None
Map: Richland Riverfront Trail - www.TrailLink.com
Trail contact: Richland Parks and Recreation: (509) 942-7529
Trailhead GPS: N46.2788 W119.2713

FINDING THE TRAILHEAD

From US 12 (I-182), take exit 5B to merge onto George Washington Way. Merge onto George Washington Way, then drive north 1.5 miles. Turn right onto Newton Street and park at the end of the road at Howard Amon Park.

WHAT TO SEE

Richland's paved, 7-mile Riverfront Trail traces the Columbia River linking several parks along the way. Part of a greater network of riverside trails in the Tri-Cities, this bite-sized river ramble is much more manageable than the 23-mile Sacagawea Heritage Trail for day-trippers and weekend visitors. The section described here blends natural scenery with urban access: you can hop on the trail at various points, splashing in the river and relaxing by the beach, all while remaining conveniently close to trailside hotels and eateries.

Begin by walking south from Howard Amon Park. An anchor of the trail accessible from downtown Richland, this park provides plenty of shaded greenspace for your urban escape. Sit on one of the swinging benches to watch the massive Columbia River roll on by, carrying all manner of vessels (including geese and the occasional tumbleweed). At the Lee Boat Dock, you might spot a large river cruise ship from as far downriver as Vancouver. Pass through the playground area, swim beach, and kids' wading pool (a winner on scorching summer days) before exiting the park.

Heading southeast from Howard Amon Park, the trail leaves behind tree cover and becomes fully exposed. Bring appropriate clothing and sunscreen on warmer days, as temperatures can get above 100 degrees in this area. Consider an early morning walk or twilight stroll along this section during warmer months. Pass by hotels, townhouses, a golf course, and private residences as you walk, with the Columbia River as your constant companion. Badger Mountain is visible along this open stretch, and you'll find the occasional interpretive sign offering information on local birds, fish, and more. Did you know, for example, that Columbia Sturgeon can live to be over 100 years old? Or that they can grow to over 1,500 pounds and 20 feet long? We didn't!

Entering the marina, you'll find more upscale hotel and dining options before crossing into Columbia Point Marina Park. Take a break at the covered picnic shelters here

A tour boat passes by Richland Riverfront on the Columbia River.

The harbor at Columbia Point Marina Park attracts private boats and cruises.

to watch riverboats come and go, refill water bottles, or have a picnic. With restrooms, a playground, and plenty of parking, Columbia Point Marina Park is another good place to start your urban hike. Extend your walk from here (see Going Further below), or return the way you came.

Going Further: From Richland Riverfront Trail's south end at Columbia Point Marina Park, you can connect to the 23-mile Sacagawea Heritage Trail for a longer walk. If you'd prefer to walk the entire 7 miles of the Richland Riverfront Trail, head north from Howard Amon Park. The trail north passes through Leslie Groves Park before terminating at USS Triton Park. Featuring the enormous sail of the USS *Triton*—the first vessel to circumnavigate the Earth submerged—this overlooked little park is worth the stop for a submarine history lesson.

MILES AND DIRECTIONS

0.0   Head south on the Richland Riverfront Trail along the Columbia River.

1.7   Use the crosswalk at the marina boat launch to enter Columbia Point Marina Park. Explore the park, then return the way you came.

LOCAL INTEREST

Monterosso's Italian Restaurant: Classy-casual Italian fare in an antique railroad dining car, with a great selection of local and Italian wines. Get the tiramisu! For beer and a more family friendly atmosphere, try their sister restaurant (Atomic Ale Brewpub) across the street. Both restaurants are a short walk from Howard Amon Park on the

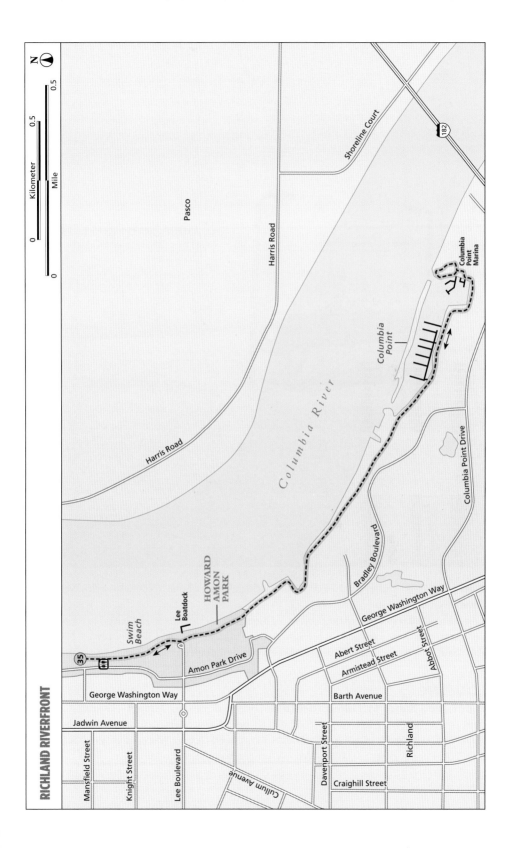

RICHLAND RIVERFRONT

N

Kilometer
0   0.5

Mile
0   0.5

Mansfield Street

Knight Street

Lee Boulevard

Cullum Avenue

Jadwin Avenue

George Washington Way

Amon Park Drive

HOWARD AMON PARK

Lee Boatdock

Swim Beach

35

Barth Avenue

Abert Street

Armistead Street

George Washington Way

Davenport Street

Craighill Street

Richland

Abbot Street

Bradley Boulevard

Columbia River

Columbia Point

Columbia Point Drive

Columbia Point Marina

Harris Road

Harris Road

Shoreline Court

Pasco

182

Swinging benches are a frequent highlight along the Riverfront Trail.

Riverfront Trail. Address: 1026 Lee Blvd., Richland, WA; Phone: (509) 946-4525; Web: www.monterossos.com

Longship Cellars: Wine tasting and small bites (think charcuterie and baked brie) on the Riverfront Trail, just south of Howard Amon Park. Address: 404 Bradley Blvd. #100, Richland, WA; Phone: (509) 713-7676; Web: www.longshipcellars.com

LODGING

Homewood Suites by Hilton Richland: Located along the Columbia River within steps of the Richland Riverfront Trail, this all-suite hotel offers a complimentary hot breakfast and weekday evening reception. Address: 1060 George Washington Way, Richland, WA; Phone: (509) 371-1550; Web: www.homewoodsuites3.hilton.com

36 BATEMAN ISLAND

Experience a leisurely walk along old farm roads while whistling to the tune of birdsong at Bateman Island. This riverside ramble is easy enough for all ages, with abundant wildlife-spotting opportunities.

Elevation gain: 20 feet
Distance: 2.1-mile lollipop
Hiking time: 1-2 hours
Difficulty: Easy
Seasons: Year round
Trail surface: Dirt path, grass, gravel
Land status: City park
Nearest town: Richland
Other users: Cyclists

Water availability: Yes, at Wye Park
Canine compatibility: Dogs must remain on leash
Fees and permits: None
Map: USGS Kennewick
Trail contact: Richland Parks and Recreation: (509) 942-7529
Trailhead GPS: N46.2382 W119.2257

FINDING THE TRAILHEAD

From US 12 E (I-182), take exit 5A to merge onto WA-240 E. Continue 1.5 miles on WA-240 E, then take the Columbia Park Trail exit. Drive 0.5 miles, then enter a traffic circle. Take the 3rd exit onto Columbia Park Trail. Drive 1.0 miles to Wye Park on the left.

WHAT TO SEE

The site of a former farm on the Columbia River, Bateman Island is named after the four Bateman brothers (Otis, Del, Charlie, and Wallace) who farmed here between 1943 and 1952. But the island's history runs much deeper. Explorer William Clark (of the Lewis and Clark Expedition) visited the island in 1805, where he traded with native tribes. Today Bateman Island provides an easy urban escape between the cities of Richland and Kennewick in the Tri-Cities.

At the trailhead parking lot in Wye Park, you'll find restrooms, water, and a playground nearby. Head north towards Bateman Island, dropping about 20 feet and crossing the Sacagawea Trail (see Going Further below). Soon you'll find yourself at the island's entrance: a gated causeway between the Yakima River Delta and the Columbia River. Signage here points out Richland's diverse wildlife, ranging from American goldfinch (Washington's official state bird) and bald eagle to coyote and western rattlesnake. Due to the rich riparian habitat, you're most likely to see (and hear) various birds here. But keep an eye out for skunks frolicking in the tall grass!

Along the tree-lined causeway, fishermen cast leisurely into the river. Enjoy peek-a-boo westerly views to Badger Mountain before beginning the island loop. Stay on the wide, soft-surface farm roads for the best walking experience as the trail alternates between dirt, gravel, and grass. The southern end of the island offers ample shade beneath both native and non-native trees. Entering the island's interior, you'll begin to notice the charred remains of tree trunks—evidence of fires that swept the island in 2001 and 2017. Fortunately, nature is forever reclaiming Bateman Island in the form of new growth.

At the north end of the island (Asparagus Point, according to the Troop 77 Girl Scout map), a small beach provides views west to Badger and Candy Mountains. You can also

Native Nootka rose grows along the path on Bateman Island.

Oleaster, or Russian olive, is an example of the noxious weeds that are starting to spread on the island.

see the Lee-Volpentest Bridges from here—a pair of bridges linking Richland and Pasco over the Columbia River. Imagine the view William Clark had here in 1805, completely devoid of modern civilization. In over 200 years since, Bateman Island has been subject to everything from turkey farming to forest fires before returning to its natural state—an undeveloped oasis between two rivers.

Complete the loop by heading south through the center of the island. You'll pass between wetland and grassland before meeting the main trail and returning to the causeway. Consider extending your hike along the paved Sacagawea Trail, or simply call it a day at just over 2 miles round trip.

Going Further: The 23-mile Sacagawea Heritage Trail offers a mostly flat, paved lollipop loop for walkers, joggers, and cyclists. From Bateman Island you can head east on the loop into Columbia Park and Clover Island before crossing the Cable Bridge into Pasco. Or head west on the Sacagawea Heritage Trail to pass through the Yakima River Delta.

MILES AND DIRECTIONS

0.0   From the parking area at Wye Park, head north through a break in the fence toward Bateman Island. Cross the Sacagawea Trail and continue north across the causeway.

0.2   Stay left at all trail junctions to hike in a clockwise direction.

0.9   Turn left at the junction.

1.0   Reach a small beach at the north end of the island. Turn around here and return to the last junction.

1.1   Turn left at the junction.

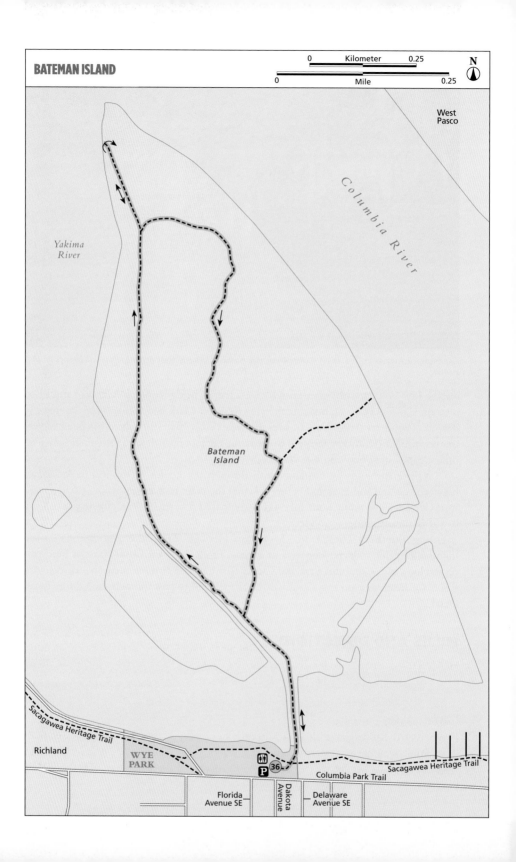

BATEMAN ISLAND

0   Kilometer   0.25

0   Mile   0.25

N

West
Pasco

Columbia River

*Yakima
River*

*Bateman
Island*

Sacagawea Heritage Trail

Richland

WYE
PARK

P 36

Sacagawea Heritage Trail

Columbia Park Trail

Florida
Avenue SE

Dakota
Avenue

Delaware
Avenue SE

Sections of the trail offer peek-a-boo views of the Columbia River.

1.7   Turn right at the junction.

1.9   Turn left to close the loop and return to the trailhead.

LOCAL INTEREST

Ice Harbor Brewing at the Marina: Chill out with award-winning Ice Harbor brews at this brewpub overlooking the Port of Kennewick on Clover Island. Their Tangerine Hefeweizen is especially refreshing on a hot day. Address: 350 N Clover Island Dr., Kennewick, WA; Phone: (509) 586-3181; Web: www.iceharbor.com

LODGING

Homewood Suites by Hilton Richland: Located along the Columbia River with Riverfront Trail access, this all-suite hotel offers a complimentary hot breakfast and weekday evening reception. Address: 1060 George Washington Way, Richland, WA; Phone: (509) 371-1550; Web: www.homewoodsuites3.hilton.com

37 BADGER MOUNTAIN

Climb through grasslands and sagebrush to the highest point in the Tri-Cities for a bird's-eye view of the Columbia River Basin.

Elevation gain: 770 feet
Distance: 3.4-mile loop
Hiking time: 2 hours
Difficulty: Moderate
Seasons: Year round
Trail surface: Gravel
Land status: County park, city park
Nearest town: Richland
Other users: Cyclists, joggers

Water availability: Yes, at restrooms
Canine compatibility: Dogs must remain on leash
Fees and permits: None
Map: Friends of Badger Mountain: www.friendsofbadger.org/trail-faq
Trail contact: Friends of Badger Mountain: (509) 783-6558
Trailhead GPS: N46.2374 W119.3071

FINDING THE TRAILHEAD

From US 12 (I-182), take exit 3A toward Queensgate South. Merge onto Queensgate Drive, and continue straight through two traffic circles. Turn left onto Keene Road and drive 0.6 miles. Turn right onto Shockley Road and drive 0.8 miles to the parking lot at Trailhead Park.

WHAT TO SEE

Badger Mountain looms 1,593 feet above the city of Richland, the highest point in the Tri-Cities. Its familiar prominence is omnipresent in skyline views from the banks of the Columbia River, and other oft-visited locations. The climb to the peak rewards hikers with an unobstructed view of the Tri-Cities and geological landmarks of the Columbia River Basin.

For many years, the trails along the ridge of Badger Mountain were popular with locals looking to get some exercise. In 2003, local residents came together to protect Badger Mountain from development. This group, Friends of Badger Mountain, is also responsible for creating and improving the current trail system.

Trailhead Park gives access to two of Badger Mountain's most popular trails: Canyon and Sagebrush. Combined, these two trails create a loop that explores two very distinctive sides of the mountain. Forgot a leash for your canine companion? Loaner leashes are provided at the trailhead in order to keep everyone safe on the trail. Not only is Badger Mountain home to a number of rattlesnakes, but many native birds nest in the grasses located near the trail. It's always best practice for dogs (and humans) to stay on-trail.

From the junction just past the leash kiosk at 0.2 mile, head south, taking the Sagebrush Trail towards the summit. The grade on this trail is gentler than that of the Canyon Trail, making for a more gradual crawl to the peak. For the first half mile, you might wonder how the Sagebrush Trail got its name—this first section winds through tall grasses, and the constant urban reminder as you peer down into the backyards of nearby residents. But after the gentle curve of one of the trail's multiple switchbacks, you'll come into a stand of mature sagebrush. Perfuming the air, the sagebrush will be your constant companion as you approach the summit.

The view of the Columbia River and Tri-Cities from Badger Mountain.

Just before reaching 1.1 miles, turn right to continue on to the summit along the Skyline Trail. Originating at the other trailhead for Badger Mountains' trail system, the Skyline Trail traces the spine of Badger's ridgeline. The trail seems a bit more rugged here, with sections of steeper grade. You'll reach the summit at 2.1 miles.

From the summit, views of the Columbia Basin spread below, the Wallula Gap visible to the southeast. You can pick out Bateman Island, jutting into the Columbia River directly ahead. And to the northwest, spot the chain of peaks: Candy, Red, and Rattlesnake Mountains respectively. Imagine that the ground under your feet was once an island, surrounded by the waters of Lake Lewis—the result of the Missoula Floods some 11,000 years ago. An ice dam broke, letting loose a torrent of water that settled in the Columbia Basin. The waters finally receded through a weak point, creating the now familiar Wallula Gap. Keep an eye out on the trail for stone markers noting the highest reach of Lake Lewis.

Admire the view and then set out on the Canyon Trail. In the spring, the hillsides of the canyon are peppered with wildflowers; balsamroot, phlox, and wild mustard are bursts of color contrasting with earth tone grasses. The rolling sides of the snaking canyon are spectacular from above, and this impressive descent into the gully makes a strong case for hiking the trail in a clockwise direction. Take advantage of the stone bench at 2.3 miles for not only rest, but an excellent viewpoint of the landscape. At 3.2 miles, you'll come to the final descent on the Canyon Trail with a set of staircases. Improvements to this section caused a temporary closure in 2019 as safer stone steps were installed. Finish the stairs and arrive back at Trailhead Park.

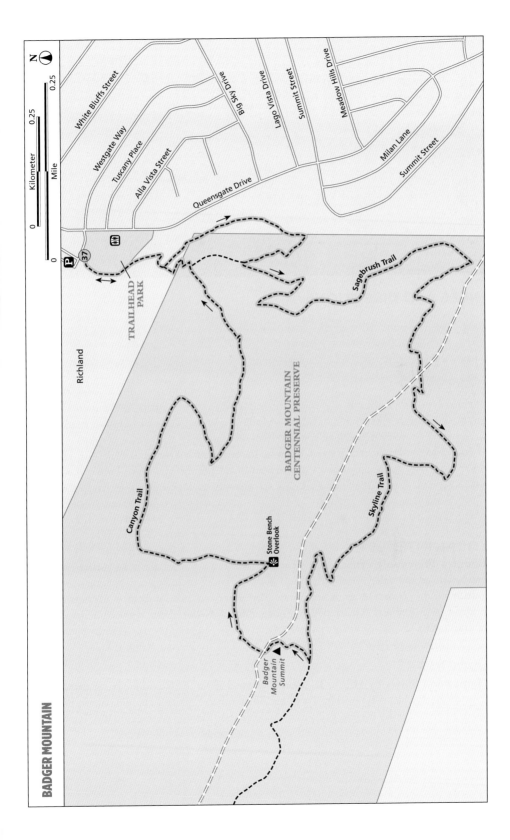

BADGER MOUNTAIN

N

0   Kilometer   0.25

0   Mile   0.25

White Bluffs Street

Westgate Way

Tuscany Place

Alla Vista Street

Big Sky Drive

Lago Vista Drive

Summit Street

Meadow Hills Drive

Milan Lane

Summit Street

Queensgate Drive

Richland

P

37

TRAILHEAD PARK

Canyon Trail

Sagebrush Trail

Skyline Trail

BADGER MOUNTAIN CENTENNIAL PRESERVE

Stone Bench Overlook

Badger Mountain Summit

From the peak, you can see neighboring Candy Mountain, Red Mountain, and Rattlesnake Mountain.

MILES AND DIRECTIONS

0.0 Begin from the southeast corner of the paved parking lot. Head south on the trail around Trailhead Park.

0.1 Reach a junction and kiosk. Continue south on the main Badger Mountain trail.

0.2 Turn left on the Sagebrush Trail.

0.5 Turn left to stay on the Sagebrush Trail.

1.1 Turn right on Skyline Trail.

1.3 Continue straight through a road junction.

2.0 Turn right to reach the summit, following the trail along the fenceline.

2.1 Turn right to descend via the Canyon Trail.

3.2 Stay left at a junction with the Sagebrush Trail. Then descend the stairs and return to the trailhead.

LOCAL INTEREST

Country Mercantile: This family owned Tri-Cities icon started as a farmstand and now offers an unrivaled selection of local gourmet goods including a deli, bakery, and homemade ice cream. A great stop before or after your hike at Badger Mountain. Address: 5015 Ava Way, Richland, WA; Phone: (509) 366-4902; Web: www.countrymercantile.com

LODGING

Homewood Suites by Hilton Richland: Located along the Columbia River within steps of the Richland Riverfront Trail, this all-suite hotel offers a complimentary hot breakfast and weekday evening reception. Address: 1060 George Washington Way, Richland, WA; Phone: (509) 371-1550; Web: www.homewoodsuites3.hilton.com

38 SPOKANE RIVER WALK LOOP

Walk several bridges over the Spokane River for views of the Upper Falls and the attractions of Expo '74 at Riverfront Park.

Elevation gain: 150 feet
Distance: 3.1-mile loop
Hiking time: 2 hours
Difficulty: Easy
Seasons: Year round
Trail surface: Paved path
Land status: City park
Nearest town: Spokane
Other users: Joggers, cyclists
Water availability: Yes, at restrooms

Canine compatibility: Dogs must remain on leash
Fees and permits: Paid parking ($5 all day)
Map: Maps and Parking - City of Spokane: www.my.spokanecity.org/riverfrontspokane/visitor-info
Trail contact: City of Spokane: (509) 625-6600
Trailhead GPS: N47.6604 W117.4212

FINDING THE TRAILHEAD

From I-90, take exit 280 for Division Street. Keep right, following signs for Division Street South, and turn right onto Division Street. Turn right immediately onto W 5th Avenue. Drive 0.3 mile, then turn right onto S Washington Street. Drive north 0.6 mile, then turn left onto W Spokane Falls Boulevard. Street parking is available along this road. For the nearest parking lot, take the first right onto N Post Street. Parking Lot 6 will be on the right ($5 all-day parking). Begin your walk from the Rotary Fountain (outside the visitor center) at the south end of the park.

WHAT TO SEE

In the heart of the city, Spokane Falls thunders from the canyon bottom of the Spokane River Gorge. Through the decades, the riverfront has undergone many changes—from its industrial past to its current life as a beloved city park. Take a stroll back in time along the river.

The first section of this urban hike takes you through the newly revamped Riverfront Park. Created for Expo '74, Riverfront Park has been a gathering place for visitors and residents of Spokane alike for over 40 years. The 1974 Expo was the first World's Fair with an environmental theme, and the park was constructed with this in mind, using the majestic Spokane River Gorge as a backdrop. The greenspace is overflowing with attractions, but nothing is more impressive than Spokane Falls, which makes it an excellent first stop.

From the visitor center and Rotary Fountain, set off across the newly constructed orange bridge and through the connections gardens towards the falls. You'll most likely hear the falls before you see them—but what a sight they are! The best views are from the South Suspension Bridge, which you'll cross on your way to snxw meneʔ (formerly Canada Island). The island was renamed snxw meneʔ (sin-HOO-men-huh) in 2017, using the Salish word for "salmon people" in honor of the Spokane Tribe. Explore the island and cross back over a set of rapids on the blue Howard Street Bridge to the main island.

The highlight of Riverfront Park is the impressive view of Spokane Falls.

Sunset is an ideal time to check out the newly renovated Pavilion.

You've seen the natural highlight of the park. Now, prepare for the man-made show-piece: The Pavilion. Built as a giant tent for Expo, the Pavilion was the site of the original IMAX screen that debuted at the exposition. The screen and walls have been removed, leaving a dizzying spiral of metallic wire. Explore the elevated walkway, especially at sunset as the golden light filters in. On weekend nights, a light show takes place inside the Pavilion, making the structure look like it's in motion.

Continue up the spine of the island to a pedestrian bridge that crosses onto the north bank of the river. Part of the Riverwalk Loop Trail, the path now continues past a number of waterfront hotels, along the placid Spokane River. As you make your way east, you'll soon enter the Gonzaga University campus. If you're feeling up to it, the campus's grounds are worth exploring as well. Round the bend in the river and cross the Don Kardong Bridge. Now on the south bank of the river, you'll be walking along the Centennial Trail. Nearly 40 miles long, the Centennial Trail continues all the way to the Washington-Idaho border. As you walk past the convention center, a number of statues and public art are on display.

Cross the wooden King Cole Bridge back to the park, and walk past the iconic Great Northern Clock Tower. The only remnant of the former railway depot, the clock tower sits peacefully on the river bank surrounded by willows, making for an elegant photo opportunity. It's hard to imagine that this lush park was once a busy industrial hub criss-crossed with train tracks. Just past the clock tower, cross the river for the final time to head back to the trailhead. Along the way, consider a visit to the Red Wagon (an over-sized Radio Flyer with slide) and the Garbage Goat. These fun attractions will delight younger hikers. Walk along the boardwalk around the historic Looff Carrousel and return back to the visitor center.

Riverfront Park's renovation will continue through at least Fall 2020, so there may well be more to explore in the coming years.

Going Further: There's plenty more to see along the Spokane River. On the west side of Riverfront Park, cross North Post Street to enter Huntington Park, where a series of stairs descends to an overlook above the Lower Falls. Or consider continuing east or

The iconic clock tower has quite the legacy starting as part of the rail depot in 1902 before becoming the centerpiece of Expo '74, and now remaining as a beloved landmark.

west on the Centennial Trail. The paved pathway is also open to bicycles, so pedaling is a great option.

MILES AND DIRECTIONS

0.0 From the Rotary Fountain (in front of the Riverfront sign and visitor center), walk north across the orange bridge.

0.1 Turn left at the signed junction for the Upper Falls.

0.2 Turn left, then turn right to cross the south suspension bridge. At the end of the bridge, walk east across snxw mene² (Canada Island).

SPOKANE RIVER WALK LOOP

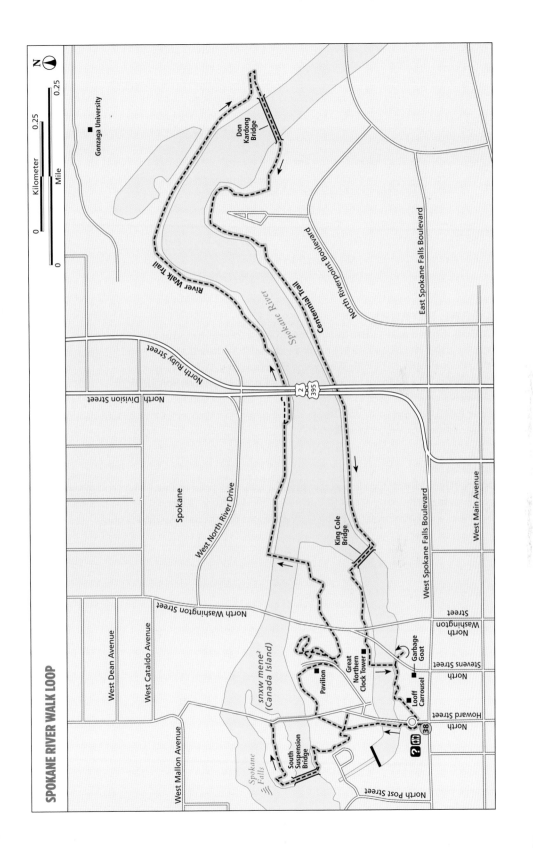

N

Kilometer
0   0.25

0   0.25
Mile

Gonzaga University

Don Kardong Bridge

River Walk Trail

Spokane River

Centennial Trail

North Ruby Street

North Division Street

2
395

Spokane

West North River Drive

North Washington Street

King Cole Bridge

West Spokane Falls Boulevard

North Riverpoint Boulevard

East Spokane Falls Boulevard

West Main Avenue

West Dean Avenue

West Cataldo Avenue

West Mallon Avenue

snxw mene² (Canada Island)

Pavilion

Great Northern Clock Tower

Garbage Goat

North Stevens Street

North Washington Street

Looff Carrousel

North Howard Street

Spokane Falls

South Suspension Bridge

North Post Street

38

2

0.4	Turn right to cross the Howard Street Promenade (blue bridge), then turn left to enter the Pavilion.
0.5	Reach the Pavilion. Ascend the ramps and steps to access the viewpoint.
0.8	After exploring the Pavilion, walk to a signed junction at the south end. Head east, toward Lilac Bowl.
0.9	Pass the Forestry Shelter, then turn left and cross the Lou Barbieri Bridge. At the end of the bridge, turn right onto the cobblestone trail.
1.2	Turn right at a junction for the pedestrian underpass beneath N Division Street.
1.9	Turn right onto the Centennial Trail and cross the pedestrian bridge over the river. Walk west on the Centennial Trail along the riverfront.
2.7	Turn right and cross the King Cole Bridge into Riverfront Park. Then turn left and walk west along the river.
2.9	Reach the Clock Tower. Turn left to cross the Clock Tower Bridge.
3.0	At the end of the bridge, turn left to reach a playground with an oversized Red Wagon. Then walk west around the Carousel to reach the trailhead.

LOCAL INTEREST

Atticus Coffee and Gifts: Inspired by *To Kill a Mockingbird*, Atticus is a great place to stop to grab a bite to eat or a hot drink for the trail. Address: 222 N Howard St., Spokane, WA; Phone: (509) 747-0336; Web: www.facebook.com/AtticusCoffee

Numerica SkyRide: Ride over the falls. Located in Riverfront Park, the SkyRide allows riders to pass over the Lower Falls in an enclosed gondola. Address: 720 W Spokane Falls Blvd, Spokane, WA; Phone: (509) 625-6600; Web: www.my.spokanecity.org/riverfrontspokane/attractions/skyride/

LODGING

Ruby River Hotel: On the river and on the trail, this spacious hotel offers comfortable rooms and easy walking access to downtown food options. Address: 700 N Division St, Spokane, WA; Phone: (509) 326-5577; Web: www.rubyriverhotelspokane.com/

39 BOWL AND PITCHER LOOP

Sporting devilish rock features and a swinging bridge over Spokane River rapids, Riverside State Park's Bowl and Pitcher area contains several of Spokane's most famous natural landmarks.

Elevation gain: 100 feet
Distance: 2.5-mile loop
Hiking time: 1–2 hours
Difficulty: Easy–Moderate
Seasons: Year round (beware of ice and snow during winter)
Trail surface: Gravel path, paved path
Land status: State park
Nearest town: Spokane
Other users: Cyclists, joggers

Water availability: Yes, at restrooms
Canine compatibility: Dogs must remain on leash
Fees and permits: Discover Pass
Map: Washington State Parks - Riverside State Park Maps: www.parks.state.wa.us/573/Riverside
Trail contact: Riverside State Park: (509) 465-5064
Trailhead GPS: N47.6959 W117.4956

FINDING THE TRAILHEAD

From I-90, take exit 280 toward Lincoln Street. Turn left onto S Walnut Street and drive 0.4 mile north on Walnut Street. Walnut becomes Maple Street. Continue north on Maple Street, crossing the Maple Street Bridge. After 0.9 mile, turn left onto W Maxwell Avenue. Drive 0.3 miles, then continue onto N Pettet Drive. Drive 0.8 mile, then take a slight left onto W Downriver Drive/N Pettet Drive/N Riverside State Park Drive. Follow this road for 3.6 miles, then turn left into the signed state park campground. Follow signs to the day-use area parking lot.

WHAT TO SEE

With 55 miles of trails spread out over 9,000 acres, it's no easy feat deciding where to walk at Riverside State Park. For first-timers (and return visitors), the Bowl and Pitcher area packs both easy access (just 6 miles from downtown Spokane) and lots of loveable features into a manageable day-trip destination. From this attractive campground, you'll gain access to an overlook 100 feet above the surging Spokane River and its massive Swinging Bridge. Big basalt boulders rise from the river, giving the area its perplexing name. Can you spot the Bowl and Pitcher? We'll show you the way.

An interpretive sign at the trailhead explains how early settlers named The Pitcher in the 1880s. By 1915 the split columnar rock (it *sort of* looks like a pitcher with a handle) became known as the Devil's Teapot—a more apt description, in our opinion. Climb to a high overlook on the east side of the river for the best Bowl and Pitcher view. Once you spot The Pitcher, look upstream 200 feet or so and you'll see a dark, concave indentation in the large boulder nearest the bridge. This is The Bowl.

Once you've surveyed the scene from on high, return to the trailhead and follow the paved, luge-like path down to the bridge. Read about the impressive bridge at an interpretive sign before crossing. Originally constructed in 1941 by the Civilian Conservation Corps (CCC), the sturdy Swinging Bridge has since been reconstructed for modern-day use. Downriver you can see The Pitcher (but not The Bowl) from the bridge. On the west side of the Spokane River, climb a set of stairs before turning north on Trail 25.

The CCC-built suspension bridge crosses over rapids in the Spokane River just upriver from the Bowl and Pitcher.

Crumbling rock piles toe up to the trail. Stick to the water for the best views, making a counterclockwise loop along the riverside. After 1 mile of walking the river calms, and fishermen can sometimes be spotted wading in the waters. The gravel path is tree-lined for shade—a pleasant walk, especially during shoulder season. Soon you'll approach more rapids at the Devil's Toenail—a rocky protrusion resembling the big toe of Lucifer himself. After a short climb, you'll reach the wide, easygoing Trail 211. Cruise south on Trail 211 to return to the Swinging Bridge and trailhead. If you'd like to extend your hike, it's possible to do so in numerous ways.

Going Further: From the Devil's Toenail, head north on Trail 211 to reach the Centennial Trail. You'll find a restroom here and miles of paved trail in either direction. At nearly 40 miles in length, the Centennial Trail begins from the northern end of Riverside State Park at the Nine Mile Recreation Area on Lake Spokane. From there, it runs through downtown Spokane along Riverfront Park (see Hike #38) all the way to the Idaho border.

Opportunities for further exploration are nearly endless within the park. Grab a park map from the trailhead kiosk or visitor center, and hike to your heart's content.

MILES AND DIRECTIONS

- **0.0** From the trailhead parking area, walk north 0.15 miles through the campground to reach the overlook. Then return to the trailhead.
- **0.3** Back at the trailhead, walk the paved path west into the picnic area.
- **0.4** Reach the suspension bridge over the Spokane River. Cross the bridge and ascend the stairs.
- **0.5** Turn right (north) onto Trail 25.
- **0.7** Reach a four-way intersection. Turn right to stay on Trail 25.
- **1.2** Stay right at the junction, following the river north.

Farther downstream, the Devil's Toenail rapids take on the appearance of a stone big toe in the middle of the Spokane River.

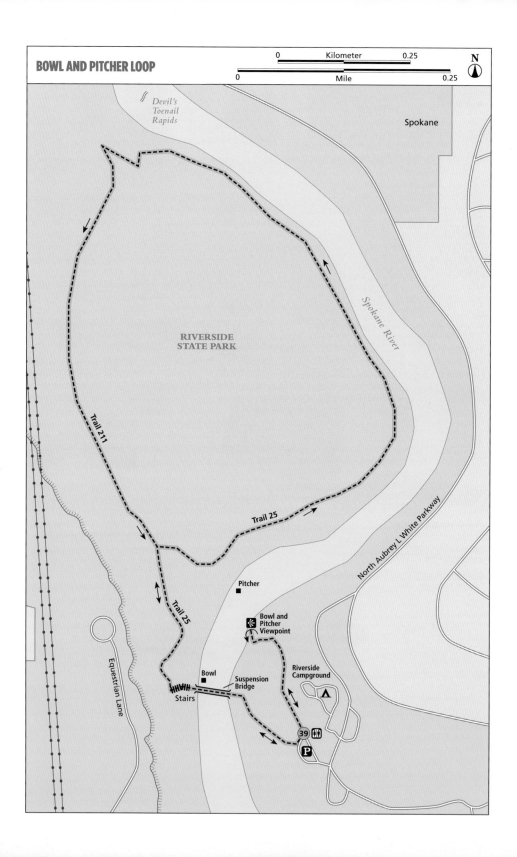

BOWL AND PITCHER LOOP

Kilometer
0   0.25

Mile
0   0.25

N

Devil's
Toenail
Rapids

Spokane

RIVERSIDE
STATE PARK

Spokane River

Trail 211

Trail 25

Trail 25

North Aubrey L White Parkway

Pitcher

Bowl and
Pitcher
Viewpoint

Riverside
Campground

Equestrian Lane

Bowl

Suspension
Bridge

Stairs

39

1.5 Reach a view of the Devil's Toenail. At the next junction, stay left and head uphill to reach Trail 211.

1.6 Turn left onto the wide Trail 211 and walk south.

2.1 Return to the four-way intersection. Continue straight (south) to retrace your steps to the trailhead.

LOCAL INTEREST

Steam Plant: Grab a beer and a bite—or simply explore the iconic former steam plant facility in downtown Spokane. Yes, you can go inside one of the smokestacks! Address: 159 S Lincoln St., Spokane, WA; Phone: (509) 777-3900; Web: www.steamplantspokane.com

LODGING

Bowl and Pitcher Campground: Laid-back state park campground near the Spokane River and miles of trails. Address: 4427 N Aubrey L White Parkway, Spokane, WA; Phone: (509) 625-5553; Web: www.parks.state.wa.us/573/Riverside

40 DISHMAN HILLS LOOP

Explore Dishman Hills Natural Area for panoramic views of Spokane Valley, cool dark ravines, and aromatic ponderosa pine forests on this loop hike.

Elevation gain: 600 feet
Distance: 3.9-mile loop
Hiking time: 2 hours
Difficulty: Moderate due to elevation gain
Seasons: Year round (beware of ice and snow during winter)
Trail surface: Dirt path, paved path
Land status: County park, natural resource conservation area
Nearest town: Spokane Valley
Other users: Joggers (bikes prohibited)

Water availability: Seasonally during summer, at Camp Caro restrooms
Canine compatibility: Dogs must remain on leash
Fees and permits: None
Map: Spokane County Parks - Dishman Hills Natural Area Trail Map: www.spokanecounty.org/Facilities/Facility/Details/Dishman-Hills-Natural-Area-32
Trail contact: Spokane County Parks: (509) 477-4730
Trailhead GPS: N47.6543 W117.2896

FINDING THE TRAILHEAD

From I-90, take exit 285 toward Sprague Avenue. Continue straight onto E Appleway Boulevard and follow it for 1.2 miles. Turn right onto Sargent Road, across the street from the Toyota dealership. Park in the large lot on the right (Camp Caro lower lot). The trail begins from the south end of the lot.

WHAT TO SEE

Criss-crossed with trails, the Dishman Hills Natural Area is ideal for a "Choose Your Own Adventure" style hike. A series of interconnected loop trails make it a favorite for locals, who are able to cycle through a route each time to the various highlights in this urban pine forest. The route described here is a highlights reel—we'll help you take in the best of the area in under 4 miles of hiking.

The Dishman Hills area is a geologic wonderland with cool ravines and large rocky bluffs cropping out of surrounding woodlands. Created by one of the state's oldest land trusts, the natural area is bordered by the cities of Spokane and Spokane Valley, offering not only recreation areas for hikers, but a home to local wildlife. It's paramount to keep your dogs on a leash in the Dishman Hills out of respect for fellow hikers and wildlife alike.

Set out from the lower parking lot towards Camp Caro Lodge, a reservable event space that includes restrooms and water. Think of Camp Caro Park as the gateway to Dishman Hills: the majority of the trails take off from the park. The first stop on your tour of the natural area is Deep Ravine. After wandering through the ponderosa forest, the ravine's walls tower above you. The trail follows the ravine's floor, creating a cooler landscape ideal for warm summer months. If you can, visit during fall or spring—not only will the temperatures be more manageable, but the ravine bursts with color. Autumn sets shrubs and trees ablaze with oranges and reds, and the spring brings the sunny joy of arrowleaf balsamroot. Rattlesnakes are also native to this area, and are more likely to be encountered late-spring through mid-fall. Just another reason to keep your pooch on a leash!

Eagle Peak offers expansive views of Spokane Valley and the surrounding mountains.

Continue hiking through the rocky ravine. After turning at the Camp Caro sign at 0.9 mile, you'll begin to climb steadily toward Eagle Peak over the next mile. Signage in Dishman Hills leaves something to be desired, so a map of the area is highly recommended, if not mandatory. As the trail starts to climb out of the forest, you'll catch a glimpse of Eagle Peak, the summit of which is reached by switch-backing up its side. From the bald peak, the views are fantastic. The neighborhoods of Spokane Valley spread out like a patchwork quilt, the foothills rising in the distance. See if you can pick out Mount Spokane!

After descending from the peak, you'll start on your way toward Nimbus Knob. Eagle Peak is the most southern point on the loop as we describe it. From this point on, if you are ever in doubt where to turn at a junction, following signs north toward Camp Caro will point you in the correct direction. Now on the Nimbus Knob Trail, you'll pass a seasonal pond before reaching the granite knob. While not quite as impressive as the view from Eagle Peak, Nimbus Knob offers a view towards the city of Spokane. Industrial sprawl and highways in the distance will put into perspective how close the city actually is.

Continue over the knob via a set of rustic stairs, hiking back through the long-needled pines towards Camp Caro. You'll lose 360 feet of elevation over the next 0.9 miles back to the trailhead. The hum of highway traffic will hit your ears once more, reminding you that despite the rugged beauty of Dishman Hills, it truly is an urban forest.

MILES AND DIRECTIONS

0.0 Walk south from the parking area to reach the Camp Caro upper parking lot (closed to public parking at the time of writing).

0.1 Proceed through the lodge breezeway to a trailhead kiosk. Turn left at the kiosk to take the Deep Ravine Loop Trail.

0.3 Turn left at a junction to make a clockwise loop. Then stay right at all junctions.

0.9 Reach the Camp Caro sign and turn right.

1.0 Stay left at the junction.

1.2 At the intersection, turn left (south) on the Goldback Trail.

1.3 Reach a trail map and turn left (east). Stay right at the next several junctions to walk south on Eagle Peak Trail.

1.9 Reach the Eagle Peak spur and turn right for Eagle Peak. Then return to the spur and turn right to make a loop.

2.2 Turn right to stay on the Eagle Peak Trail. Stay left at the next trail junction.

2.6 After passing a dry pond area, turn right for the Nimbus Knob Trail.

3.0 Reach Nimbus Knob. Continue northwest on the Nimbus Knob Trail.

3.2 Turn right on the Pond Loop Trail. Stay right at the next junction.

3.4 Turn left (north) to stay on the Pond Loop Trail. Stay right at the following junctions.

3.7 Stay right at two junctions, then proceed through the fence and turn left on the paved path. Follow this path back to the Camp Caro upper parking lot and retrace your steps to the trailhead.

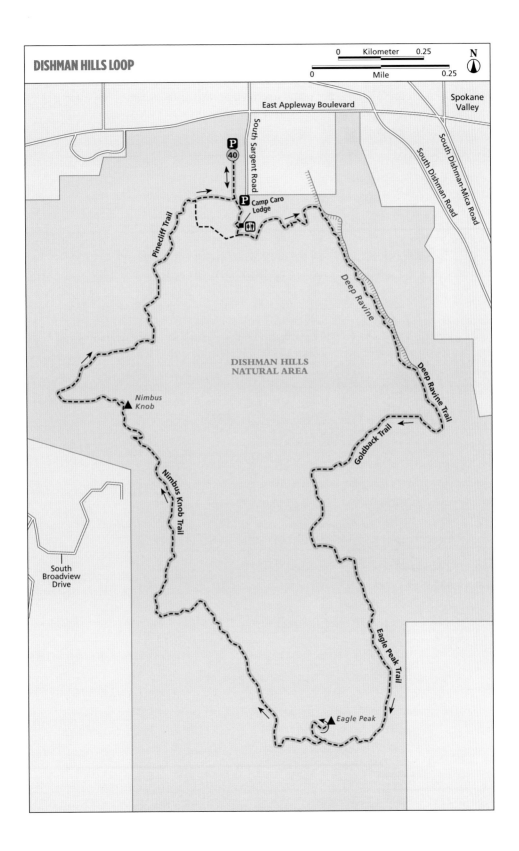

DISHMAN HILLS LOOP

East Appleway Boulevard

Spokane
Valley

South Sargent Road

P
40

P Camp Caro
Lodge

South Dishman-Mica Road

South Dishman Road

Pinecliff Trail

Deep Ravine

DISHMAN HILLS
NATURAL AREA

Deep Ravine Trail

Nimbus
Knob

Goldback Trail

Nimbus Knob Trail

South
Broadview
Drive

Eagle Peak Trail

Eagle Peak

Breathtaking in the fall, Dishman Hills is a great shoulder-season hike.

LOCAL INTEREST

Hopped Up Brewing Company: Set in an old pancake house, this family friendly, Hot Rod-themed brewery is right down the street from Dishman Hills and a great place to kick back after a hike. Address: 10421 E Sprague Ave., Spokane Valley, WA; Phone: (509) 413-2488; Web: www.hoppedupbrew.com

LODGING

Holiday Inn Express Spokane Valley: Just off I-90 and a few miles from Dishman Hills, this hotel is close to Spokane Valley restaurants. Address: 9220 E Mission Ave., Spokane, WA; Phone: (509) 927-7100; Web: www.ihg.com

HIKE INDEX

MEET YOUR GUIDES

Brandon Fralic and **Rachel Wood** are the authors of *Beer Hiking Pacific Northwest*, the first guidebook pairing trails and ales in Washington, Oregon, and British Columbia. Since launching their blog *Beers at the Bottom* in 2013, they've contributed to *Washington Trails*, *REI Coop Journal*, *OutdoorsNW*, and other outlets together. Both lifelong Washingtonians, they grew up hiking, camping, and exploring their home state.

Brandon lives in Bellingham, WA, where he is the craft beer blogger for *Bellingham Tourism*. His travel writing has appeared in numerous publications including *Northwest Travel & Life*, *Scenic Washington*, and *Outdoor Project*. Rachel lives in Kirkland, WA, and earned a master's degree in creative writing. She's worked in the craft beer industry since 2015 and currently works at a neighborhood brewery. Follow Brandon and Rachel on social media @beersatb and on their website: www.beersatthebottom.com.

THE TEN ESSENTIALS OF HIKING

American Hiking Society

American Hiking Society recommends you pack the "Ten Essentials" every time you head out for a hike. Whether you plan to be gone for a couple of hours or several months, make sure to pack these items. Become familiar with these items and know how to use them. Learn more at **AmericanHiking.org/hiking-resources**

1. Appropriate Footwear

2. Navigation

3. Water (and a way to purify it)

4. Food

5. Rain Gear & Dry-Fast Layers

6. Safety Items (light, fire, and a whistle)

7. First Aid Kit

8. Knife or Multi-Tool

9. Sun Protection

10. Shelter